BUDAPEST GUIDE 2023 AND BEYOND

Exploring Budapest's Historic Splendor, Thermal Baths, Parliament, and Hungarian Cuisine

Aliz Kristof

Copyright © 2023 Aliz Kristof

All rights reserved.

Without the proper written consent of the publisher and copyright owner, this book cannot be used or distributed in any way, shape, or form, except for brief quotations used in a review. This book should not be considered a substitute for medical, legal, or other professional advice.

CONTENTS

INTRODUCTION	i
GET TO KNOW BUDAPEST	1
Origin and History of Budapest	1
Visa Requirements	4
Currency	5
Language	6
Weather	6
Travel Insurance	7
Public Transportation	9
Safety	11
Tap Water	12
Tipping	13
Cultural Etiquette	14
Dress Code	16
Opening Hours	17
Emergency Numbers	19
WHAT TO SEE	20
Budapest Ferris Wheel	20
Chain Bridge	21
Thermal Baths	23
Heroes' Square	26
Andrassy Avenue	28
Margaret Island Water Tower	30
Vajdahunyad Castle	32
Danube River Cruises	34
Margaret Bridge	36
Citadella	39
WHERE TO STAY	42
Popular Locations	42
Lucury Accomodations	43
Budget Accomodations	45
WHAT & WHERE TO EAT	47
What to eat	47
Where to eat	49
Best Restaurants	52
BUDAPEST ARCHITECTURE	55
Buda Castle	56
Hungarian Parliament	58
Széchenyi Chain Bridge	60
Gellért Baths	62
St. Stephen's Basilica Architecture	64
Dohány Street Synagogue	66
Great Market Hall (Nagyvásárcsarnok)	68
Hungarian State Opera House	70
Vajdahunyad Castle Architecture	72
Budapest Palace of Arts (Müpa Budapest)	74
The Innovative Whale (Bálna Budapest)	76

MONUMENTS AND STATUES	79
Imre Nagy Memorial	79
Steve Jobs Memorial Statue	81
Army Statues	83
The Statue of Liberty (Szabadság Szobor)	84
Shoes on the Danube Bank	86
Matthias Fountain (Mátyás Kútja)	88
Anonymous Statue (Ismeretlen Írók Tere)	89
Little Princess (Kiskirálylány)	90
Ronald Reagan Statue	92
Ferenc Liszt Monument	94
BUDAPEST MARKETS	97
Hold Street Market Hall (Hold utcai Piac)	97
Great Market Hall	99
Lehel Market (Lehel tér)	101
Ecseri Flea Market (Ecseri Piac)	103
Fény Street Market (Fény utcai Piac)	104
BUDAPEST MUSEUMS	107
Hungarian National Museum	107
Museum of Fine Arts	109
Hungarian National Gallery	111
Museum of Applied Arts	113
Holocaust Memorial Center	115
House of Terror	117
Hospital in the Rock Nuclear Bunker Museum	119
BUDAPEST TUNNELS	122
Buda Castle Labyrinth	123
Szemlőhegyi Cave	125
Tunnel under Castle Hill	127
Millennium Underground	129
Batthyány Square Metro Station	131
Déli Railway Station Tunnel	132
BUDAPEST CHURCHES	135
St. Stephen's Basilica (Szent István Bazilika)	135
Matthias Church (Mátyás-templom)	137
Great Synagogue (Dohány Street Synagogue)	140
St. Anne's Church (Szent Anna-templom)	141
St. Michael's Church (Szent Mihály-templom)	143
Church of Our Lady (Boldogasszony-templom) in Óbuda	145
St. Elizabeth of Hungary Church (Erzsébet-templom)	147
ECLECTIC NEIGHBORHOODS	149
District VII (Erzsébetváros)	149
District VIII (Józsefváros)	149
District IX (Ferencváros)	150
District XIII (Újlipótváros)	150
District VI (Terézváros)	150
District V (Belváros-Lipótváros)	150
STREET ART AND GRAFFITI	151
District VII (Jewish Quarter)	151
Kazinczy Street	153
Gozsdu Courtyard	155
Ruin Bars Street Art	157
Urban Art Galleries	159

Street Art Festivals	161
BARS AND NIGHTLIFE	164
Ruin Bars	164
Pub Crawls	165
Live Music Venues	167
Széchenyi Thermal Bath Night Spa	169
Rooftop Bars	171
Clubbing Scene	172
EVENTS AND FESTIVALS	175
Budapest Advent Fair	175
Budapest Spring Festival	177
Budapest Wine Festival	179
Sziget Festival	181
Budapest International Documentary Festival (BIDF)	183
Budapest Pride	185
National Gallop	186
Formula 1 Hungarian Grand Prix	188
Budapest Christmas Tram	190
MAPS	192
Budapest Map	192
Sziget Festival Map	193
Budapest Christmas Market Map	194
Budapest Museums Map	195
Széchenyi Thermal Bath map	196
Restaurants Map	197
ITINERARIES	198
Historical and Cultural Exploration (3 Days)	198
Family-Friendly Fun (4 Days)	199
Culinary Delights (2 Days)	200
Romantic Getaway (3 Days)	201
Budget-Friendly Budapest (4 Days)	202
CONCLUSION	204
INDEX	205

INTRODUCTION

Welcome to Budapest, a city of rich history, breathtaking architecture, and vibrant culture. As you embark on your journey through this enchanting Hungarian capital, prepare to be captivated by its historic splendor, rejuvenating thermal baths, magnificent Parliament building, and delectable Hungarian cuisine. Budapest seamlessly blends old-world charm with modern allure, creating a unique destination that caters to all kinds of travelers. Whether you're a history buff, a food enthusiast, or simply seeking relaxation, Budapest has something special in store for you. Let's delve into this comprehensive travel guide to discover the wonders of Budapest in 2023 and beyond.

GET TO KNOW BUDAPEST

Before you go to Budapest, Hungary, here are some important things to keep in mind to make your trip smooth and enjoyable:

Origin and History of Budapest

The origin and history of Budapest is a fascinating tale of two cities, Buda and Pest, that eventually merged to form the modern capital of Hungary. Here's a brief overview of the origin and historical development of Budapest:

Ancient Settlements

The area around present-day Budapest has been inhabited since ancient times. Celtic tribes settled in the region around 1st century BC, followed by the Romans who established the town of Aquincum in the 1st century AD. Aquincum was an important Roman provincial capital and played a significant role in the Roman Empire's administration.

Conquering of Hungary

In the 9th century, the region came under the rule of the Hungarians, who founded the Hungarian Kingdom. During this period, the Magyar tribes established the fortress of Buda on the western bank of the Danube River, while Pest, on the eastern bank, began to develop as a trading center.

Royal Capital

Buda became the seat of Hungarian kings, and the town gradually expanded into a significant medieval city. It was fortified with walls, and several notable buildings, including Buda Castle and Matthias Church, were constructed.

Turkish Occupation

In the 16th century, the Ottoman Empire conquered Buda and ruled over the city for over 150 years. During this time, many of the city's churches and buildings were converted into mosques, leaving a lasting impact on its architectural heritage.

Rebuilding and Development

After the liberation from the Ottoman rule in the late 17th century, Buda and Pest began to rebuild and prosper under the Habsburg rule. The Austrian Empress Maria Theresa played a crucial role in the city's development, commissioning various architectural projects.

Unification of Buda and Pest

The unification of Buda and Pest as a single city began in 1873, along with the incorporation of Óbuda (Old Buda). The new city, named Budapest, became the capital of Hungary and quickly developed into a thriving cultural and industrial center.

20th Century

Budapest experienced significant events in the 20th century, including World War I and World War II, both of which left their mark on the city. During World War II, Budapest suffered severe damage and was occupied by Nazi Germany and later by Soviet forces.

Post-War Reconstruction

After the war, Budapest underwent extensive reconstruction efforts. Many historic buildings were restored, and new structures were added, contributing to the city's unique architectural blend of old and modern elements.

Transition to Democracy

In the late 20th century, with the fall of communism in Hungary and the end of the Soviet era, Budapest transitioned to a democratic system. The city saw rapid economic growth and development, becoming a popular tourist destination and a center for commerce, education, and culture.

Today

Budapest stands as a vibrant and cosmopolitan European capital, known for its stunning architecture, thermal baths, rich cultural heritage, and captivating history that reflects the layers of civilizations that have shaped its identity over the centuries.

Visa Requirements

Hungary is a member of the European Union and part of the Schengen Area. If you are a citizen of a country that is part of the Schengen Area, you generally do not need a visa to enter Hungary for short stays (up to 90 days within a 180-day period) for tourism, business, or family visits.

Citizens of the following countries do not need a visa to enter Hungary for short stays:

- All EU/EEA member states (European Union/European Economic Area)
- Switzerland, Norway, Iceland, and Liechtenstein (Schengen Area countries but not EU members)
- Andorra, Monaco, San Marino, and Vatican City (Microstates with a special visa exemption)

If you are a citizen of a country that is not part of the Schengen Area, you may need to apply for a Schengen visa to enter Hungary or any other Schengen country. The Schengen visa allows you to travel freely within the Schengen Area during the validity of the visa.

It's essential to check the specific visa requirements based on your nationality and the purpose of your visit. Visa regulations can change over time, so it's advisable to consult the official website of the Hungarian embassy or consulate in your country or the official website of the Hungarian Ministry of Foreign Affairs for the most up-to-date information on visa requirements and application procedures.

Currency

The official currency of Hungary is the Hungarian Forint (HUF). It is abbreviated as "Ft" or "HUF." The forint is further divided into 100 smaller units called fillér, but the use of fillér coins has been largely discontinued, and most prices are now quoted in forints only.

When traveling to Hungary, it's essential to have some Hungarian Forints with you for day-to-day expenses, especially in smaller establishments and markets where credit cards might not be accepted. You can exchange your currency to Hungarian Forints at banks, currency exchange offices, or ATMs (automated teller machines) located throughout the country.

Most major credit cards (Visa, MasterCard, American Express, etc.) are widely accepted in hotels, restaurants, shops, and tourist attractions in Budapest and other major cities. However, it's always a good idea to carry some cash for smaller purchases or in case you encounter places that do not accept cards.

Before your trip, check with your bank about any foreign transaction fees or international withdrawal fees that may apply when using your credit or debit card abroad. Also, inform your bank about your travel plans to avoid any issues with your card while in Hungary.

Language

The official language of Hungary is Hungarian, also known as Magyar. Hungarian is a unique language with no direct linguistic relations to neighboring languages, making it one of the more challenging languages to learn for foreigners.

The Hungarian language uses the Latin alphabet, and while it might seem complex at first, learning a few basic phrases and expressions can be helpful and appreciated during your visit to Hungary.

While Hungarian is the primary language spoken in Hungary, you will find that English is widely spoken and understood, especially in tourist areas, hotels, restaurants, and among the younger population. In addition to English, you may also encounter people who speak German, French, or other European languages, particularly in areas with high international tourist traffic.

When traveling to Hungary, knowing a few basic Hungarian phrases such as "hello" (szia), "thank you" (köszönöm), and "goodbye" (viszontlátásra) can be a friendly way to engage with locals and enhance your cultural experience. Even if your Hungarian is limited, most Hungarians are friendly and welcoming to visitors, and you should be able to navigate the country comfortably with English as your primary language.

Weather

Budapest experiences a temperate continental climate with four distinct seasons, each offering a different experience for visitors. Here's an overview of the weather in Budapest throughout the year:

Spring (March to May)

Spring in Budapest is a lovely time to visit as the city comes alive with blooming flowers and greenery. The weather is generally mild, with average daytime temperatures ranging from 10°C to 20°C (50°F to

68°F). It's a good idea to bring layers, as temperatures can fluctuate during the day and evenings might still be a bit chilly.

Summer (June to August)

Summer is the peak tourist season in Budapest, attracting visitors with its warm and sunny weather. Daytime temperatures can reach 25°C to 30°C (77°F to 86°F) and occasionally even higher. It's an excellent time for outdoor activities, exploring the city's parks, and enjoying the Danube River cruises. However, be prepared for occasional heatwaves, and stay hydrated during hot days.

Autumn (September to November)

Autumn in Budapest is a beautiful season with mild weather and colorful foliage. Daytime temperatures range from 10°C to 20°C (50°F to 68°F) in the early part of the season but gradually cool down as November approaches. It's a pleasant time for sightseeing, and the city is less crowded compared to the summer months.

Winter (December to February)

Winter in Budapest can be cold, with temperatures ranging from -1°C to 5°C (30°F to 41°F) during the day, and often dropping below freezing at night. Snowfall is common, especially in January and February, creating a picturesque winter landscape. The holiday season adds a magical touch with festive markets and decorations throughout the city. Warm clothing and layers are essential if you plan to visit Budapest during winter.

Travel Insurance

Travel insurance is a type of insurance that provides coverage and financial protection against unexpected events that may occur during your travels. It is designed to offer you peace of mind and financial security while you are away from home. Travel insurance typically covers various aspects of your trip, including:

Trip Cancellation or Interruption

If you need to cancel or cut short your trip due to unforeseen circumstances such as illness, injury, or a family emergency, travel insurance can help reimburse you for non-refundable trip expenses.

Medical Expenses

Travel insurance can cover medical expenses incurred while traveling, including emergency medical treatment, hospitalization, and evacuation.

Baggage and Personal Belongings

Travel insurance can provide compensation if your baggage is lost, stolen, or damaged during your trip.

Travel Delay

If your trip is delayed due to circumstances beyond your control (e.g., flight cancellation, severe weather), travel insurance can help cover additional expenses such as accommodation and meals.

Emergency Assistance

Travel insurance often includes access to 24/7 emergency assistance services, providing support and guidance in case of emergencies during your trip.

Accidental Death and Dismemberment

Travel insurance may provide a benefit in the event of accidental death or serious injury during your travels.

Before purchasing travel insurance, carefully review the policy's terms, coverage limits, exclusions, and any optional add-ons or upgrades. Some travel insurance policies may have specific restrictions or exclusions related to pre-existing medical conditions, adventure activities, and certain types of travel.

It's important to buy travel insurance as soon as you book your trip, as some benefits, such as trip cancellation coverage, may only apply if you purchase the insurance within a certain time frame after making your initial trip deposit.

Travel insurance is highly recommended, especially for international trips or trips with significant non-refundable expenses. It provides valuable protection against unexpected events that could disrupt or impact your travel plans.

Public Transportation

Budapest has an efficient and extensive public transportation system that makes it easy to get around the city. The public transportation network includes buses, trams, metro lines, trolleybuses, and suburban railway services. Here's what you need to know about public transportation in Budapest:

Tickets and Fares

You can use the same ticket for all types of public transportation within the city (bus, tram, metro, and trolleybus). Tickets can be purchased at ticket vending machines located at metro stations, major bus and tram stops, and some newspaper kiosks. You can also buy tickets from the driver on buses and trams. It's essential to validate your ticket before boarding and keep it with you during your journey, as ticket inspections are common.

Types of Tickets

Budapest's public transportation offers various ticket types, including single tickets, 24-hour tickets, 72-hour tickets, 7-day passes, and monthly passes. Depending on the duration of your stay and how often you plan to use public transportation, you can choose the most suitable option.

Metro

Budapest's metro system consists of four lines (M1, M2, M3, and M4). The metro is one of the fastest ways to travel between different parts of the city, especially during rush hours.

Trams and Buses

Budapest has an extensive tram and bus network, covering most areas of the city. Trams are especially popular for sightseeing as they often pass by major landmarks and offer scenic routes along the Danube River.

Suburban Railway (HÉV)

The suburban railway lines connect Budapest with neighboring towns and villages. They are useful for reaching destinations outside the city center.

Night Transportation

Budapest also has a night bus network that operates during the late hours when the regular public transportation is not available.

Budapest Card

If you plan to use public transportation extensively and visit multiple attractions, consider getting the Budapest Card. It provides unlimited travel on public transportation and offers free or discounted entry to many museums, sights, and attractions.

Accessibility

Budapest's public transportation system is generally accessible for people with disabilities, with elevators and ramps available at many metro stations and low-floor buses on some routes.

Safety

Budapest is generally considered a safe city for travelers, with a low crime rate compared to other major European cities. However, like any destination, it's essential to take some precautions to ensure a safe and enjoyable trip. Here are some safety tips for your visit to Budapest:

Watch Your Belongings

Pickpocketing can occur in crowded tourist areas, public transportation, and popular attractions. Be mindful of your belongings and avoid carrying large sums of cash or valuable items in easily accessible pockets.

Stay in Well-Lit Areas

While Budapest is generally safe, it's advisable to stay in well-lit and busy areas, especially at night. Avoid poorly lit streets or alleys, particularly if you are traveling alone.

Use Licensed Taxis

If you need a taxi, use licensed and reputable taxi companies. Avoid accepting rides from unmarked or unofficial taxis, as they may overcharge or take advantage of tourists.

Be Cautious at Night

Budapest's nightlife is vibrant, but it's essential to be cautious, especially after consuming alcohol. Stick to well-known bars, clubs, and busy areas, and avoid accepting drinks from strangers.

Emergency Numbers

Memorize or keep handy the emergency numbers for Hungary. The general emergency number is 112, which connects you to police, fire, and medical assistance.

Respect Local Laws and Customs

Familiarize yourself with local laws and customs to avoid unintentionally offending locals or getting into legal trouble.

Public Transportation Safety

Budapest's public transportation is generally safe, but be cautious of your surroundings, especially during rush hours when pickpocketing can occur.

Scams and Tourist Traps

Be aware of common tourist scams, such as overcharging for goods or services. Avoid street vendors selling counterfeit items and be cautious when exchanging money at unofficial currency exchange offices.

Trust Your Instincts

If something feels off or unsafe, trust your instincts and remove yourself from the situation.

Tap Water

In Budapest, the tap water is generally safe to drink. Hungary has stringent water quality standards, and the tap water undergoes regular testing to ensure its safety for consumption. The water treatment facilities in Budapest meet high-quality standards, making the tap water safe, clean, and free of harmful substances.

Locals regularly drink tap water without any issues, and it is commonly served in restaurants and cafes. Using tap water for brushing teeth, cooking, and other everyday activities is also safe and recommended.

The taste of tap water can vary slightly depending on the specific area within Budapest, but it is generally considered safe and of good quality throughout the city.

If you prefer, you can also buy bottled water from supermarkets and convenience stores, but it is not necessary for health reasons. Opting for tap water is not only cost-effective but also environmentally friendly, as it reduces plastic waste associated with bottled water consumption.

Overall, you can confidently enjoy the tap water in Budapest without any concerns about its safety.

Tipping

Tipping customs in Budapest and Hungary, in general, are similar to those in many other European countries. Tipping is generally appreciated, but it is not obligatory. Here are some guidelines on tipping in Budapest:

Restaurants and Cafes

In restaurants and cafes, it is common to leave a tip if you are satisfied with the service. A tip of around 10% of the total bill is considered a polite gesture. Some establishments may include a service charge in the bill, so it's a good idea to check before adding an additional tip.

Bars

In bars, it's customary to round up the bill or leave a small tip for the server or bartender, especially if you received good service.

Taxis

Tipping taxi drivers is not mandatory, but it is common to round up the fare or add a small tip if you were pleased with the service.

Tour Guides

If you participate in guided tours or excursions, it's customary to tip the tour guide as a token of appreciation for their services. A tip of a few euros per person is considered a thoughtful gesture.

Hotel Staff

It's not obligatory to tip hotel staff, but leaving a small amount for the housekeeping staff is a kind gesture if they provided good service during your stay.

Other Services

For other services, such as hairdressers or spa treatments, tipping is optional and typically not included in the final bill.

Cultural Etiquette

When visiting Budapest and Hungary, it's essential to be aware of cultural etiquette to show respect for local customs and traditions. Here are some cultural etiquette tips to keep in mind:

Greetings

Hungarians generally greet each other with a firm handshake, maintaining eye contact. Use formal titles (e.g., Mr., Mrs., or Dr.) when addressing people until invited to use their first names.

Politeness

Politeness is highly valued in Hungarian culture. Remember to say "please" (kérem) and "thank you" (köszönöm) when making requests or receiving assistance.

Body Language

Avoid standing with your hands in your pockets, as it is considered impolite. When crossing your legs, be mindful not to display the sole of your shoe towards someone, as it is seen as disrespectful.

Toasting

In social gatherings, it's common to make toasts with alcoholic beverages. When toasting, maintain eye contact with others and clink glasses. Traditionally, Hungarians say "egészségedre" (pronounced "eg-esh-shay-ged-reh"), which means "to your health."

Dining Etiquette

When invited to someone's home for a meal, it's customary to bring a small gift for the host, such as flowers or a box of chocolates. Wait for the host to invite you to sit at the table, and remember to keep your hands visible during the meal, resting them on the table.

Public Behavior

Avoid raising your voice or speaking loudly in public places, as it can be perceived as rude. Respect queues and wait your turn when in lines.

Dress Code

In general, Hungarians dress modestly and conservatively. When visiting churches or other religious sites, dress appropriately, covering your shoulders and knees.

Tipping

Tipping is appreciated but not obligatory. Leave a tip for good service in restaurants and other service establishments, but it is not expected in all situations.

Language

Learn a few basic Hungarian phrases to greet and thank people. Hungarians appreciate the effort of foreigners to speak their language.

Religion

Hungary has a predominantly Christian population, and religious customs and traditions are respected. When visiting churches or religious sites, show appropriate reverence and dress modestly.

Dress Code

Budapest is a cosmopolitan city with a relaxed and diverse dress code. As a tourist, you can feel comfortable wearing casual and smart-casual attire for most activities and attractions. However, there are a few situations where dressing appropriately is recommended:

Sightseeing and Daily Activities

For exploring the city, visiting museums, and strolling around, casual and comfortable clothing is suitable. Jeans, shorts, t-shirts, blouses, and comfortable shoes are perfect for everyday activities.

Dining at Restaurants

Budapest has a vibrant culinary scene, and most restaurants have a casual to smart-casual dress code. While there is no strict requirement, dressing slightly more formal, such as with slacks and a collared shirt or a nice dress, is appropriate for upscale or fine-dining establishments.

Visiting Churches and Religious Sites

When visiting churches or religious sites, especially during mass or other religious ceremonies, it's respectful to dress modestly. This means covering your shoulders and knees, and avoiding revealing or beachwear-type clothing.

Thermal Baths

If you plan to visit the famous thermal baths in Budapest, remember to bring swimwear or a swimsuit. Most thermal baths require swimwear, and some baths may have specific regulations regarding swim caps.

Opera and Theater

For attending opera, theater, or other cultural performances, it's common to dress more formally. Men often wear suits or dress shirts and ties, while women opt for dresses or elegant attire.

Nightlife

Budapest has a vibrant nightlife scene with a mix of casual and upscale venues. Dress codes may vary depending on the establishment, so it's best to check beforehand. Some clubs and bars may have specific dress requirements, especially for special events.

Seasons

Be mindful of the weather and pack accordingly. Budapest experiences distinct seasons, with hot summers and cold winters. Bring appropriate clothing, such as light and breathable fabrics for summer and warm layers for winter visits.

Opening Hours

Opening hours for businesses and attractions in Budapest can vary, but here are some general guidelines:

Shops and Stores

Most shops and stores in Budapest are open from Monday to Saturday. The typical opening hours are from around 10:00 AM to 6:00 PM. Some larger shopping malls and supermarkets might stay open until later in the evening, around 8:00 PM or 9:00 PM. On Sundays, many smaller shops are closed, but larger shopping malls and souvenir shops in tourist areas may remain open.

Restaurants and Cafes

Restaurants and cafes in Budapest usually open around 11:00 AM for lunch and continue serving until late evening. Many restaurants close briefly in the late afternoon and reopen for dinner. Some cafes may have longer hours, staying open into the evening for drinks and desserts.

Museums and Attractions

Museums and attractions in Budapest generally have varying opening hours, but they typically open around 10:00 AM and close in the early evening, around 5:00 PM or 6:00 PM. Some museums might be closed on Mondays, so it's a good idea to check their specific schedules in advance.

Banks

Banks in Budapest are usually open from Monday to Friday, from 8:00 AM to 4:00 PM. Some larger bank branches might have extended hours or be open on Saturday mornings.

Pharmacies

Pharmacies in Budapest typically have regular business hours, but some of them offer 24-hour service on a rotating basis. Look for signs indicating which pharmacy is open during the night or on Sundays.

Nightlife

Budapest has a vibrant nightlife scene, and many bars, clubs, and entertainment venues stay open until the early hours of the morning, especially on weekends.

Emergency Numbers

In Hungary, including Budapest, the emergency number for all types of emergencies is 112. Dialing 112 will connect you to the emergency services, including police, fire, medical assistance, and other emergency response teams.

When calling the emergency number, it's important to remain calm and provide clear and concise information about the nature of the emergency, your location, and any other relevant details. The operators on the other end of the line are trained to handle emergencies and will dispatch the appropriate emergency services to assist you.

It's a good idea to memorize or save the emergency number 112 in your phone contacts before your trip to Hungary, as it is the same number used throughout the European Union for emergencies. Whether you need immediate medical attention, report a crime, or require assistance in any emergency situation, 112 is the number to call.

WHAT TO SEE

Budapest Ferris Wheel

Explore the city from new heights with the Budapest Ferris Wheel. Standing tall at 65 meters, it proudly claims the title of Europe's largest ferris wheel. Erected by the same company responsible for La Grande Roue in Paris, the Budapest Eye operates year-round, offering visitors a thrilling ride and spectacular views of the city.

Located at the heart of Budapest on Erzsébet Square, the Ferris Wheel is a prominent landmark that can be seen from afar, towering above the surrounding buildings. From the top, you'll be treated to breathtaking panoramas that encompass iconic sights like St. Stephen's Cathedral, the Hungarian Parliament, and the UNESCO World Heritage Site Andrássy Avenue.

The cabins are partially open, providing a unique experience as you soar above the cityscape. If you're not afraid of heights and want to capture unforgettable memories, don't miss the opportunity to take a ride on this giant wheel.

Operating daily from 10:00 am to midnight, a single ride lasts approximately 8-10 minutes, during which the wheel completes three turns. Tickets can be purchased on-site, with prices at 2400 HUF (around 8 euros) for adults and 1500 HUF (around 5 euros) for children aged 2 to 14.

During peak seasons, be prepared for potential queues, but the incredible panoramic view of Budapest is more than worth the wait.

Chain Bridge

The Chain Bridge, also known as Széchenyi Chain Bridge, is one of Budapest's most iconic landmarks and a symbol of the city. It spans the Danube River, connecting the Buda and Pest sides of Budapest. Here's more information about the Chain Bridge:

History

The Chain Bridge was the first permanent bridge built across the Danube in Budapest. It was designed by English engineer William Tierney Clark and completed in 1849. The bridge played a significant role in connecting the two separate cities of Buda and Pest, contributing to the unification of Budapest as a single entity.

Architecture

The Chain Bridge is a masterpiece of engineering and architectural elegance. It features a suspension design with massive stone pillars at each end and iron chains supporting the roadway. The bridge's iconic lion statues, known as the Bridge Guardians, guard each entrance and have become a symbol of the city.

Panoramic Views

Walking or driving across the Chain Bridge provides breathtaking views of the Danube River, the Parliament Building, Buda Castle, and the Pest side's stunning architecture. The best time to enjoy the panoramic views is during sunset or at night when the city is beautifully illuminated.

Pedestrian Walkway

The Chain Bridge has a dedicated pedestrian walkway on both sides of the road, allowing visitors to enjoy a leisurely stroll while taking in the city's scenic beauty. Walking across the bridge offers a unique perspective of Budapest's architectural wonders.

Illumination

The Chain Bridge is beautifully illuminated at night, adding to the city's enchanting atmosphere. The bridge's lights reflect on the Danube River, creating a mesmerizing view that is a highlight of Budapest's evening skyline.

Danube River Cruises

The Chain Bridge is a popular starting point for Danube River cruises. Numerous cruise companies offer scenic boat tours along the river, allowing you to admire Budapest's landmarks from a different perspective. Cruising under the Chain Bridge is a memorable experience.

Festivals and Events

The Chain Bridge serves as a backdrop for various cultural events and festivals throughout the year. It is often used as a focal point for fireworks displays during celebrations like New Year's Eve or the August 20th fireworks show, commemorating Hungary's national holiday.

Thermal Baths

Budapest is famous for its thermal baths, which are not only a popular attraction but also an integral part of Hungarian culture and a source of relaxation and well-being. Here's some information about the thermal baths in Budapest:

Széchenyi Thermal Bath

Located in City Park (Városliget), Széchenyi Thermal Bath is one of the largest and most famous thermal baths in Budapest. It features a mix of indoor and outdoor pools with varying temperatures, including thermal pools, saunas, steam rooms, and medicinal baths. The bath's beautiful yellow Neo-Baroque architecture adds to its charm.

Gellért Thermal Bath

Situated in the Gellért Hotel, Gellért Thermal Bath is known for its stunning Art Nouveau architecture and elegant interior. The bath complex offers a range of thermal pools, including indoor and outdoor pools, effervescent baths, and various spa and wellness services. Don't miss the opportunity to relax in the famous Gellért Bath's thermal wave pool.

Rudas Baths

With a history dating back to the 16th century, Rudas Baths offer a unique and more traditional bathing experience. The bath features an

Ottoman-style octagonal pool, as well as several other thermal pools, steam rooms, and saunas. Rudas Baths also have a rooftop pool with panoramic views of Budapest.

Király Baths

Király Baths is one of the oldest thermal baths in Budapest, dating back to the 16th century during the time of the Ottoman Empire. The bath has retained its traditional Turkish architecture and atmosphere, offering visitors an authentic and historic bathing experience. Király Baths features thermal pools, steam rooms, and saunas.

Lukács Baths

Lukács Baths, located on the Buda side of Budapest, is another historic thermal bath. It has been in operation since the 19th century and is known for its medicinal waters. Lukács Baths offer various thermal pools, saunas, and wellness services, along with a tranquil garden area.

Thermal Bath Etiquette

When visiting the thermal baths, it's important to be aware of local customs and etiquette. It is customary to shower before entering the pools, and swimwear is required in most areas. Some baths have separate days or sections for men and women, while others have mixed-gender areas. Be sure to check the specific rules and regulations of each bath before your visit.

Additional Tips

Don't forget to bring your own towel, swimsuit, and flip-flops or water shoes. Many baths also offer additional services like massages and spa treatments, which can be a great way to enhance your relaxation experience. It's advisable to arrive early in the day or book in advance to avoid crowds, especially during peak tourist seasons.

Heroes' Square

Heroes' Square, or Hősök tere in Hungarian, is a significant landmark and one of the most visited squares in Budapest. Located at the end of Andrássy Avenue, it serves as a gateway to the City Park (Városliget) and holds great historical and cultural significance. Here's more information about Heroes' Square:

History and Design

Heroes' Square was built in 1896 to commemorate the 1,000th anniversary of the arrival of the Magyars (Hungarian tribes) in the Carpathian Basin. The square's design features a large semicircular colonnade with statues of important historical figures and leaders of Hungary.

Millennium Monument

Dominating the center of Heroes' Square is the Millennium Monument, an imposing column topped with the Archangel Gabriel holding the Hungarian Crown and the apostolic double cross. The column stands as a symbol of Hungary's independence and sovereignty.

Statues and Pillars

The semicircular colonnades on either side of the square are adorned with statues of prominent historical figures and national heroes. These statues represent the seven Magyar chieftains and other key leaders who played a significant role in Hungarian history. The pillars also bear reliefs depicting important events and periods in Hungary's history.

Tomb of the Unknown Soldier

At the base of the Millennium Monument, you'll find the Tomb of the Unknown Soldier, which serves as a memorial to honor those who sacrificed their lives for Hungary. The flame burns continuously as a symbol of remembrance.

Museum of Fine Arts and Hall of Art

On either side of Heroes' Square, you'll find two important cultural institutions. The Museum of Fine Arts (Szépművészeti Múzeum) houses an extensive collection of European art, including works by renowned artists such as Raphael, Rembrandt, and Monet. The Hall of Art (Műcsarnok) is an exhibition hall that showcases contemporary art and hosts temporary art exhibitions.

City Park (Városliget)

Heroes' Square serves as the entrance to the vast City Park, a popular recreational area in Budapest. In the park, you'll find various attractions, including Vajdahunyad Castle, the Széchenyi Thermal Bath, the Budapest Zoo, and the Municipal Circus.

Events and Festivals

Heroes' Square is often a venue for national celebrations, festivals, concerts, and public gatherings. It hosts important events such as the August 20th fireworks display, Hungary's national holiday commemorating the foundation of the state.

Andrassy Avenue

Andrássy Avenue, or Andrássy út in Hungarian, is a historic boulevard located in Budapest, Hungary. It is a UNESCO World Heritage site and one of the city's most prestigious and elegant thoroughfares. Here's more information about Andrássy Avenue:

History and Design

Andrássy Avenue was constructed in the late 19th century to connect the city center with the City Park (Városliget). It was designed to be a grand boulevard, modeled after famous European avenues like the Champs-Élysées in Paris. The avenue's architecture and atmosphere reflect the wealth and grandeur of the period.

Architecture

Andrássy Avenue showcases a diverse range of architectural styles, including neo-renaissance, neo-baroque, and art nouveau. The buildings along the avenue feature beautiful facades, intricate detailing, and ornate decorations. Many of these structures house embassies, upscale shops, cafes, and cultural institutions.

State Opera House

One of the most iconic landmarks on Andrássy Avenue is the Hungarian State Opera House. Designed by renowned Hungarian architect Miklós Ybl, the Opera House is a stunning example of neo-renaissance architecture. It is not only an important cultural institution but also a popular venue for opera and ballet performances.

Hungarian University of Fine Arts

Located on Andrássy Avenue, the Hungarian University of Fine Arts (formerly the Royal Drawing School) is an esteemed institution for art education. The building itself is an architectural gem, featuring a beautiful courtyard and artistic elements.

Museums

Andrássy Avenue is home to several notable museums. The House of Terror Museum, situated in the former headquarters of the communist secret police, explores the dark history of Hungary under Nazi and Soviet rule. The Liszt Ferenc Memorial Museum, dedicated to the renowned Hungarian composer Franz Liszt, offers insights into his life and works.

Shops and Cafes

Andrássy Avenue is lined with upscale shops, boutiques, and designer stores. It is a popular destination for luxury shopping, fashion, and high-end brands. The avenue also features charming cafes and restaurants, where visitors can enjoy a leisurely break and soak up the elegant atmosphere.

Andrassy Avenue Promenade

Andrássy Avenue is not only a major thoroughfare but also a pleasant pedestrian promenade. Strolling along the avenue allows you to appreciate its architecture, admire the tree-lined boulevard, and immerse yourself in the vibrant ambiance of Budapest.

Aliz Kristof

Margaret Island Water Tower

The Margaret Island Water Tower, also known as Margitsziget Víztorony in Hungarian, is a prominent landmark located on Margaret Island (Margitsziget) in the Danube River, Budapest, Hungary. Margaret Island is a popular recreational area in the city, and the water tower is one of its notable features. Here are some key details about the Margaret Island Water Tower:

Location

The Margaret Island Water Tower is situated in the heart of Margaret Island, a lush and picturesque island in the Danube River, located between Buda and Pest. The island is a favorite destination for locals and tourists alike, offering beautiful parks, gardens, and recreational facilities.

Historical Background

The water tower was constructed in the early 20th century as part of the island's infrastructure to supply water to the city of Budapest.

Architectural Style

The Margaret Island Water Tower showcases an elegant, neo-Romanesque architectural style, which was popular during the period it was built. It features characteristic arches and decorative elements, adding to its visual appeal.

Water Supply

In the past, the tower played a vital role in storing and distributing water to Budapest. However, with advancements in water supply infrastructure, its original purpose has evolved.

Viewing Platform

Today, the water tower has been renovated and repurposed. It now serves as a viewing platform, providing visitors with panoramic views of the surrounding Margaret Island and the Budapest skyline.

Attractions Nearby

In addition to the water tower, Margaret Island offers a variety of attractions, including beautiful gardens, musical fountains, sports facilities, and historical sites.

Access

The Margaret Island Water Tower is easily accessible on foot or by renting bicycles on the island. Visitors can explore the tower and enjoy the island's serene and natural surroundings.

Vajdahunyad Castle

Vajdahunyad Castle, or Vajdahunyad vára in Hungarian, is a stunning castle complex located in Budapest's City Park (Városliget). It is a remarkable architectural ensemble that showcases various architectural styles and serves as a popular tourist attraction. Here's more information about Vajdahunyad Castle:

History

Vajdahunyad Castle was originally built in 1896 as part of the Millennial Exhibition held to celebrate the 1,000th anniversary of the Hungarian settlement in the Carpathian Basin. The castle was initially made of wood and cardboard but proved to be so popular that it was reconstructed with permanent materials in 1908.

Architectural Styles

The castle complex represents an eclectic mix of architectural styles, with each section designed to mimic famous buildings from different periods of Hungarian history. It includes elements of Romanesque, Gothic, Renaissance, and Baroque architecture. The most prominent section is a replica of the Hunyad Castle in Transylvania, hence the name "Vajdahunyad" Castle.

Castle Design and Features

Vajdahunyad Castle features a central courtyard surrounded by several wings and towers, each representing a different architectural style. The castle's intricate details, soaring towers, and charming bridges create a fairytale-like atmosphere. The buildings are made of stone and brick, lending an air of authenticity to the architectural replicas.

Museum of Hungarian Agriculture

The castle houses the Museum of Hungarian Agriculture, which offers a fascinating insight into Hungary's agricultural history and rural traditions. The museum's exhibits include agricultural tools, machinery, folk costumes, and interactive displays. Visitors can learn about the country's farming practices and the role of agriculture in Hungarian culture.

Boating Lake

Vajdahunyad Castle is situated next to a picturesque boating lake, which transforms into an ice-skating rink during the winter months. The lake provides a tranquil setting for leisurely walks, boat rides, or simply enjoying the surrounding scenery.

Events and Festivals

The castle complex and its surrounding park often host various events and festivals throughout the year. These events include concerts, cultural celebrations, craft fairs, and food festivals, providing opportunities to experience Hungarian traditions and entertainment.

Photography Opportunities

Vajdahunyad Castle offers plenty of photo opportunities with its stunning architecture and picturesque surroundings. The castle's towers, bridges, and reflections in the boating lake create captivating scenes that are ideal for capturing memorable shots.

Danube River Cruises

Danube River cruises are a popular and scenic way to explore Budapest and other cities along the Danube River. Cruising along the river allows you to admire the beauty of the surrounding landscapes, enjoy panoramic views of iconic landmarks, and experience the charm of the riverfront cities. Here's more information about Danube River cruises:

Budapest Sightseeing

A Danube River cruise in Budapest offers a unique perspective of the city's famous landmarks, including the Hungarian Parliament Building, Buda Castle, Matthias Church, and the Chain Bridge. The cruise provides an excellent opportunity to see these attractions from a different vantage point and capture stunning photos.

River Routes

Danube River cruises cover various routes, allowing you to explore different cities and regions. Popular routes include Budapest to Vienna, Budapest to Bratislava, and Budapest to Belgrade. Each route offers its own set of attractions and highlights, giving you a chance to discover multiple destinations along the way.

Day and Evening Cruises

Danube River cruises are available during the day and in the evening. Daytime cruises provide optimal visibility for sightseeing and allow you to enjoy the river and its surroundings. Evening cruises offer a romantic atmosphere, with the illuminated landmarks creating a magical setting. Some cruises also feature live music or dinner options.

Riverbank Landmarks

Besides Budapest, Danube River cruises pass by several other notable landmarks along the way. This includes the Wachau Valley in Austria, known for its picturesque vineyards and charming towns, the stunning Melk Abbey, the baroque city of Bratislava in Slovakia, and the Iron Gates, a dramatic gorge on the border of Serbia and Romania.

Riverboat Amenities

River cruise boats are equipped with various amenities to ensure your comfort and enjoyment. Most boats feature indoor and outdoor seating areas, panoramic windows, onboard restaurants or cafes, and sometimes even entertainment options like live music or cultural performances. Some larger boats may have additional amenities such as swimming pools, spas, and fitness centers.

Multilingual Guides

Danube River cruises typically provide multilingual guides who offer commentary and insights about the landmarks and history of the regions you pass through. They provide interesting information about the cities, landmarks, and cultural highlights, enhancing your overall experience.

Seasonal Considerations

Danube River cruises operate throughout the year, but the timing and availability may vary depending on the season and weather conditions. Spring and summer are popular seasons for cruising due to pleasant weather and longer daylight hours. However, cruises are also available during fall and winter, offering a different perspective with potential festive experiences during the holiday season.

Margaret Bridge

Margaret Bridge, or Margit híd in Hungarian, is a beautiful bridge that spans the Danube River in Budapest, Hungary. It connects the Buda and Pest sides of the city, offering both practical transportation and scenic views. Here's more information about Margaret Bridge:

History

Margaret Bridge was constructed between 1872 and 1876, making it one of the oldest bridges in Budapest. It was named after Princess Margaret, daughter of King Béla IV, who lived in a nearby convent on Margaret Island.

Architecture

Designed by French engineer Ernest Goüin, Margaret Bridge features a combination of iron and stone in its structure. It is a classic bridge with elegant arches and stone pillars adorned with decorative elements. The bridge's design is reminiscent of the French Second Empire style.

Connecting Buda and Pest

Margaret Bridge connects the neighborhoods of Buda, on the west bank of the Danube, with Pest, on the east bank. It spans approximately 637 meters (2,090 feet) in length and provides an important link between the two sides of the city.

Margaret Island Access

Margaret Bridge is an important access point to Margaret Island (Margitsziget). Pedestrian pathways on the bridge allow visitors to easily reach the island on foot or by bicycle. The island is a popular recreational area with parks, gardens, and attractions such as the Palatinus Thermal Baths and the Water Tower.

Scenic Views

Margaret Bridge offers breathtaking views of Budapest's skyline and the Danube River. From the bridge, you can enjoy panoramic vistas of landmarks like the Hungarian Parliament Building, Buda Castle, and the Fisherman's Bastion. The bridge itself is a picturesque sight, especially when illuminated at night.

Tram and Traffic

Margaret Bridge accommodates vehicular traffic, including cars, buses, and trams. It is an important transportation route, connecting key areas of Budapest. Trams running on Margaret Bridge provide a convenient means of getting around the city, offering scenic views during the journey.

Walking and Cycling

Margaret Bridge has designated pedestrian and bicycle lanes, making it accessible for walkers and cyclists. The pathways allow visitors to enjoy leisurely strolls or bike rides while taking in the views of the Danube and the city.

Citadella

The Citadella, also known as the Citadel, is a historic fortress located atop Gellért Hill in Budapest, Hungary. It is a prominent landmark that offers panoramic views of the city and the Danube River. Here's more information about the Citadella:

History

The Citadella was built in the mid-19th century by the Habsburg Empire as a strategic military stronghold to suppress any potential uprisings in Budapest. Its construction came after the failed Hungarian Revolution of 1848-1849. The fortress was used as a garrison and housed cannons aimed at the city.

Location and Architecture

Situated on Gellért Hill, the Citadella sits at an elevation of 235 meters (771 feet) above the Danube River. It features a pentagonal shape and large walls made of stone. The fortress includes a central courtyard, ramparts, and lookout points.

Panoramic Views

The Citadella is known for its stunning panoramic views of Budapest. From its vantage point, visitors can enjoy breathtaking vistas of the Danube River, the Hungarian Parliament Building, Buda Castle, Margaret Island, and the Pest side of the city. The Citadella offers a unique perspective and is especially popular for capturing photos of Budapest's skyline.

Liberty Statue

Within the Citadella complex stands the Liberty Statue (Szabadság Szobor), a prominent symbol of freedom and independence. The statue, erected in 1947, commemorates the liberation of Hungary from Nazi occupation during World War II.

Walks and Hiking

Gellért Hill and the Citadella are accessible by foot, allowing visitors to enjoy a scenic walk or hike. There are several paths leading to the fortress, and along the way, you can explore the picturesque park and enjoy the natural surroundings. The walk to the Citadella is uphill but can be a rewarding experience.

Citadella Park

The area surrounding the Citadella is known as Citadella Park, offering a peaceful green space with benches and picnic spots. It is a popular destination for locals and tourists seeking a tranquil setting to relax or enjoy a picnic while taking in the panoramic views.

Cultural Events and Exhibitions

The Citadella occasionally hosts cultural events, exhibitions, and open-air concerts during the summer months. These events provide an opportunity to enjoy live music, performances, and cultural displays against the backdrop of the fortress and the cityscape.

WHERE TO STAY

Popular Locations

Budapest offers a wide range of accommodations to suit different budgets and preferences. Here are some popular areas to consider for your stay in Budapest:

District V (Belváros-Lipótváros)

This central district is located on the Pest side of the city and is home to many major attractions, including the Hungarian Parliament, St. Stephen's Basilica, and the Danube River. It offers a variety of hotels, from luxury options to more budget-friendly choices. Staying in District V allows for easy access to sightseeing, shopping, dining, and nightlife.

District VII (Erzsébetváros)

Known as the Jewish Quarter, District VII is a vibrant and trendy neighborhood with a mix of historic charm and contemporary culture. It is filled with unique cafes, ruin bars, street art, and a lively nightlife scene. This district is a popular choice for those looking for a vibrant atmosphere and a taste of Budapest's alternative culture.

District VI (Terézváros)

Located next to District VII, District VI is another central area with a mix of residential and commercial areas. It is known for its elegant architecture, wide boulevards, and upscale shops. District VI is a great choice for those who want a more relaxed atmosphere while still being close to major attractions and amenities.

Castle District (District I)

Situated on the Buda side of the city, the Castle District offers a charming and historic setting. It is home to Buda Castle, Matthias Church, and Fisherman's Bastion, providing stunning panoramic views of the city. Staying in this area offers a quieter ambiance and easy access to major attractions, though it is further away from the bustling city center.

City Park (Városliget)

Located in Pest, near Heroes' Square and the Széchenyi Thermal Baths, City Park offers a tranquil environment with ample green spaces. It is a great option for those who want to stay close to the park's attractions, such as Vajdahunyad Castle and the Budapest Zoo.

Danube Promenade

The Danube Promenade, which stretches along the Pest side of the Danube River, offers stunning views of the Chain Bridge, Buda Castle, and the river itself. It is a convenient location, with easy access to major landmarks, restaurants, and river cruises. Hotels along the Danube Promenade often provide breathtaking views of the city's skyline.

Lucury Accomodations

If you're looking for luxury accommodations in Budapest, the city offers several high-end hotels and luxury properties that provide exceptional services, elegant surroundings, and a range of upscale amenities. Here are a few luxury accommodations in Budapest that are worth considering:

Four Seasons Hotel Gresham Palace

Located on the Pest side of the city, overlooking the Danube River and the Chain Bridge, the Four Seasons Hotel Gresham Palace is a renowned luxury hotel housed in a beautifully restored Art Nouveau building. It features luxurious rooms and suites, a spa and wellness center, a rooftop terrace with panoramic views, and fine dining options.

The Ritz-Carlton, Budapest

Situated in the heart of Budapest on Erzsébet tér, The Ritz-Carlton offers luxurious accommodations with stylish decor, marble bathrooms, and stunning views of the city. The hotel features a spa, fitness center, gourmet dining options, and personalized services to ensure a memorable stay.

Corinthia Hotel Budapest

This grand hotel, located on Erzsébet körút, combines historic elegance with modern luxury. The Corinthia Hotel Budapest features lavishly designed rooms, an impressive spa and wellness center with a pool, multiple dining options, and a beautiful atrium-style lobby.

Kempinski Hotel Corvinus Budapest

Located in the city center, near Vörösmarty Square, Kempinski Hotel Corvinus Budapest offers luxurious accommodations with contemporary design and a range of amenities. The hotel features an extensive spa and fitness center, several restaurants and bars, and spacious, well-appointed rooms and suites.

Aria Hotel Budapest

Situated near St. Stephen's Basilica, the Aria Hotel Budapest is a boutique luxury hotel with a musical theme. The hotel offers stylish and individually designed rooms, a rooftop garden with panoramic views, a music library, and an on-site restaurant with live piano performances.

Budget Accomodations

If you're looking for budget accommodations in Budapest, there are several options available that offer comfortable and affordable stays. Here are a few suggestions for budget-friendly accommodations in Budapest:

Hostels

Budapest has a wide range of hostels that cater to budget travelers. These establishments provide dormitory-style accommodations with shared facilities, such as bathrooms and common areas. Some popular hostels in Budapest include Maverick City Lodge, Wombats City Hostel Budapest, and Carpe Noctem Vitae.

Budget Hotels

There are also budget hotels in Budapest that offer affordable rates while still providing comfortable rooms and basic amenities. Examples of budget-friendly hotels include Hotel Erzsébet City Center, Hotel Rum Budapest, and Hotel Palazzo Zichy.

Guesthouses and Apartments

Renting a guesthouse or apartment can be a cost-effective option for travelers, especially for those staying for an extended period or traveling in groups. Websites like Airbnb, Booking.com, and VRBO offer a variety of budget-friendly guesthouses and apartments in Budapest.

Budget-Friendly Neighborhoods

Consider staying in districts that are known for having more affordable accommodations, such as District VII (Erzsébetváros) and District VIII (Józsefváros). These neighborhoods offer a vibrant atmosphere, with access to restaurants, cafes, and nightlife, while still providing affordable lodging options.

Timing and Seasonal Deals

Keep an eye out for seasonal deals and promotions offered by hotels and accommodations in Budapest. Rates may be more affordable during certain periods, such as weekdays or off-peak travel seasons.

WHAT & WHERE TO EAT

Hungarian cuisine is known for its rich flavors, hearty dishes, and unique culinary traditions. Influenced by its geographical location and historical connections, Hungarian cuisine features a combination of ingredients and techniques from neighboring countries, such as Austria, Turkey, and the Balkans, while maintaining its distinct character. Here are some key aspects of Hungarian cuisine:

What to eat

When it comes to Hungarian cuisine, there are several traditional dishes that you should try during your visit to Budapest. Here are some must-try Hungarian dishes:

Goulash (Gulyás)

Goulash is perhaps the most iconic Hungarian dish. It is a hearty meat stew, traditionally made with beef, onions, paprika, and various vegetables. It is typically seasoned with Hungarian spices and slow-cooked to achieve a rich and flavorful dish.

Langos

Langos is a popular Hungarian street food. It is a deep-fried flatbread topped with various savory ingredients, such as sour cream, grated cheese, garlic butter, and sometimes even sausages or vegetables. Langos is crispy on the outside and soft on the inside, offering a delicious and satisfying snack.

Paprikás Csirke (Chicken Paprikash)

Chicken paprikash is a classic Hungarian dish. It consists of chicken pieces cooked in a creamy paprika-infused sauce, typically served with egg noodles or dumplings called nokedli. The rich flavors of the paprika and the tender chicken make this dish a true comfort food.

Hortobágyi Palacsinta

Hortobágyi palacsinta is a savory pancake dish filled with a seasoned mixture of ground meat, onions, and spices. The filled pancakes are then rolled up, baked, and topped with a rich tomato sauce. It is a delicious and satisfying dish, often served with sour cream.

Dobos Torte

Dobos torte is a classic Hungarian cake consisting of multiple thin layers of sponge cake, sandwiched together with chocolate buttercream, and topped with a caramel layer. It is a rich and indulgent dessert, perfect for those with a sweet tooth.

Kürtőskalács

Kürtőskalács, also known as chimney cake, is a popular Hungarian sweet treat. It is made by wrapping a strip of dough around a cylindrical spit, baking it over an open flame, and then coating it with sugar or cinnamon. The result is a crispy, caramelized, and flavorful pastry that is often enjoyed with a cup of coffee.

Pörkölt

Pörkölt is a traditional Hungarian meat stew, similar to goulash but typically made without the addition of vegetables. It is often prepared with pork or beef, cooked in a rich and savory sauce, flavored with onions, paprika, and other spices. Pörkölt is commonly served with potatoes or nokedli.

Where to Eat

Budapest offers a wide range of dining options, from traditional Hungarian restaurants to international cuisines and trendy eateries. Here are some recommendations on where to eat in Budapest:

Central Market Hall (Nagyvásárcsarnok)

The Central Market Hall is not only a great place to shop for fresh produce and local products but also to sample traditional Hungarian dishes. You'll find food stalls offering authentic Hungarian specialties such as goulash, lángos, and chimney cake.

District VII (Erzsébetváros)

The Jewish Quarter in District VII is known for its vibrant food scene. Explore the area and discover unique restaurants, trendy cafes, and ruin bars serving a mix of Hungarian and international cuisines. It's a great neighborhood to try street food, fusion dishes, and traditional Jewish cuisine.

Gozsdu Udvar

Located in District VII, Gozsdu Udvar is a vibrant and lively courtyard filled with restaurants, bars, and cafes. It offers a wide range of dining options, from traditional Hungarian cuisine to international flavors and street food. It's a popular spot for both locals and tourists to enjoy a meal or grab a drink.

Raday Street

Raday Street, located in District IX, is known for its bustling restaurant scene. It's a pedestrian-friendly street with numerous dining establishments, including Hungarian restaurants, cafes, and wine bars. It's a great place to explore and find a restaurant that suits your taste.

Andrassy Avenue

This iconic avenue is lined with elegant buildings and high-end shops, and it's also home to several upscale restaurants. You'll find a variety of cuisines, including Hungarian, Mediterranean, and international options. It's a great area to enjoy a leisurely meal and indulge in fine dining experiences.

Danube Promenade

Along the Danube River, you'll find several restaurants and cafes with scenic views of the river and the city skyline. It's a picturesque setting to enjoy a meal while taking in the beautiful surroundings. Many of these establishments serve a mix of Hungarian and international dishes.

Váci Street

Váci Street is a popular shopping street in the city center, lined with restaurants, cafes, and confectioneries. It's a bustling area with a mix of tourist-friendly restaurants and local eateries. You can find a range of cuisines here, from Hungarian to Italian, Asian, and more.

Best Restaurants

Budapest is a vibrant city with a diverse culinary scene offering a wide range of dining experiences. The best restaurants in Budapest can vary depending on individual tastes and preferences, but here are some highly regarded restaurants that have received positive reviews from locals and tourists alike:

Onyx

This Michelin-starred restaurant offers a modern take on Hungarian cuisine, using high-quality ingredients and innovative techniques to create exceptional dishes.

Borkonyha WineKitchen

Renowned for its excellent wine selection and gourmet cuisine, Borkonyha WineKitchen combines the best of Hungarian and international dishes.

Costes

Another Michelin-starred restaurant, Costes, presents contemporary European cuisine with a focus on Hungarian flavors and seasonal ingredients.

Kispiac Bisztró

Serving traditional Hungarian cuisine with a modern twist, Kispiac Bisztró is known for its cozy atmosphere and hearty dishes.

Mák Bistro

Mák Bistro offers a fusion of Hungarian and international flavors in an elegant setting, making it a popular choice for fine dining.

Rosenstein Restaurant

Specializing in Jewish-Hungarian cuisine, Rosenstein Restaurant is famous for its traditional dishes and warm hospitality.

Zeller Bistro

Zeller Bistro provides a relaxed atmosphere and serves Hungarian comfort food with a focus on local, seasonal ingredients.

Menza

Menza offers a retro-chic setting and a menu featuring modern interpretations of classic Hungarian dishes.

New York Café

Although primarily known for its opulent and historic interior, the New York Café also offers a wide array of delicious cakes, pastries, and classic Hungarian dishes.

Great Market Hall

While not a traditional restaurant, the Great Market Hall (Nagyvásárcsarnok) is a fantastic place to sample various Hungarian dishes, including local specialties, street food, and fresh produce.

BUDAPEST ARCHITECTURE

Buda Castle

Buda Castle, also known as the Royal Palace or Budapest Castle, is a historical landmark located on Castle Hill in the Buda side of Budapest. It is one of the city's most significant and iconic attractions. Here's more information about Buda Castle:

History

Buda Castle has a rich history dating back to the 13th century when it was initially constructed as a fortress. Over the centuries, it underwent various reconstructions and expansions, eventually becoming the royal residence of Hungarian kings and queens.

Architecture

The castle complex showcases a mix of architectural styles, including Gothic, Renaissance, and Baroque influences. The most prominent feature is the stunning Matthias Church (also known as the Church of Our Lady) with its colorful tiled roof and intricate details.

Hungarian National Gallery

Buda Castle is home to the Hungarian National Gallery, which houses a vast collection of Hungarian art from the Middle Ages to the present. Visitors can admire paintings, sculptures, and other artworks that provide insights into Hungary's artistic heritage.

Budapest History Museum

Within the castle complex, you'll also find the Budapest History Museum. This museum offers exhibitions that explore the city's history from Roman times to the present day, providing a comprehensive overview of Budapest's development and cultural heritage.

Castle Hill District

Buda Castle is situated in the Castle Hill District, a UNESCO World Heritage site. This area is known for its charming medieval streets, historic buildings, and breathtaking views of the Danube River and the Pest side of the city. Take some time to wander through the cobblestone streets and discover hidden gems, such as the Fisherman's Bastion and the Hospital in the Rock.

Changing of the Guard

Witness the ceremonial changing of the guards at the main entrance of Buda Castle, which takes place at regular intervals. It's a traditional and picturesque event that adds to the castle's allure.

Panoramic Views

Buda Castle offers stunning panoramic views of Budapest. Don't miss the opportunity to enjoy the breathtaking vistas of the Danube River, the Chain Bridge, and the Pest side from various vantage points within the castle complex.

Hungarian Parliament

The Hungarian Parliament Building, also known as the Parliament of Budapest or the Hungarian Parliament, is one of the most iconic landmarks in Budapest and a symbol of Hungary's rich history and democracy. Here's more information about the Hungarian Parliament:

Architecture

The Hungarian Parliament Building is an architectural masterpiece and one of the largest parliamentary buildings in the world. It was designed by Hungarian architect Imre Steindl in the Gothic Revival style, inspired by the British Houses of Parliament. The building features intricate details, pointed arches, tall spires, and a prominent central dome that reaches a height of 96 meters (315 feet).

Location

Situated on the banks of the Danube River, the Hungarian Parliament Building stands on the Pest side of Budapest. Its strategic location offers panoramic views of the river and the Buda Castle on the opposite side.

Historical Significance

The Hungarian Parliament Building has a significant historical and political role. It houses the National Assembly of Hungary, where the country's elected representatives gather to discuss and make legislative decisions. The building has witnessed important moments in Hungarian history, including the proclamation of the Republic of Hungary in 1946 and the restoration of Hungary's independence in 1989.

Guided Tours

Visitors have the opportunity to explore the interior of the Hungarian Parliament through guided tours. The guided tours offer insights into the building's history, architecture, and the functioning of Hungary's parliamentary system. Highlights include the magnificent central hall, the dome, the grand staircase, and the Hungarian Crown Jewels, which are on display.

Crown Jewels

The Hungarian Crown Jewels, including the Holy Crown of Hungary, are safeguarded within the Parliament Building. These artifacts hold great significance as symbols of Hungary's sovereignty and are considered the country's most precious treasures.

Evening Illumination

The Hungarian Parliament Building is beautifully illuminated at night, creating a stunning visual spectacle. The illuminated facade highlights the building's architectural details and makes for a captivating sight, especially when viewed from the Danube River or the nearby bridges.

Kossuth Square

The Hungarian Parliament is located on Kossuth Square, a spacious square in front of the building. The square is often used for public gatherings, demonstrations, and events. It offers a great vantage point to admire the Parliament Building and take photographs.

Széchenyi Chain Bridge

The Széchenyi Chain Bridge, commonly known as the Chain Bridge, is an iconic and historically significant bridge that spans the Danube

River in Budapest, Hungary. It is one of the most famous landmarks in the city and serves as a vital transportation link between the Buda and Pest sides of Budapest. Here are some key features of the Széchenyi Chain Bridge:

Construction

The Chain Bridge was the first permanent bridge to be built across the Danube in Budapest. Construction began in 1839 and was completed in 1849. It was designed by the British engineer William Tierney Clark and built by the Scottish engineer Adam Clark.

Architecture

The Chain Bridge's design is a beautiful example of 19th-century engineering and architectural ingenuity. It features a suspension bridge design with two massive stone pillars at each end, connected by iron chains supporting the roadway.

Lion Statues

The bridge is flanked by grand stone lion statues at each of its entrances. These sculptures, designed by János Marschalkó, serve as symbols of strength and guardians of the city.

Chain Bridge Illumination

At night, the Chain Bridge is beautifully illuminated, creating a magical and romantic atmosphere along the Danube River. Its lights add to the city's charm and make it a popular spot for evening strolls.

Panoramic Views

The Chain Bridge offers breathtaking views of Budapest's major landmarks, including the Hungarian Parliament Building on the Pest side and Buda Castle on the Buda side.

Walking and Driving

The bridge is accessible to both pedestrians and vehicular traffic. Walking across the bridge provides a fantastic opportunity to appreciate its architectural details and enjoy the picturesque surroundings.

Historical Significance

The Chain Bridge played a crucial role in connecting the previously separate cities of Buda and Pest, uniting them into the modern city of Budapest. It significantly contributed to the city's development and economic growth.

Reconstruction

The Chain Bridge underwent several renovations and reconstructions over the years, the most recent major renovation taking place in 2020 to restore its structural integrity and historical charm.

Gellért Baths

The Gellért Baths, also known as Gellért Thermal Bath and Swimming Pool, is one of the most famous and historically significant thermal baths in Budapest, Hungary. Located on the Buda side of the city, at the foot of Gellért Hill, the Gellért Baths is renowned for its stunning Art Nouveau architecture, therapeutic thermal waters, and elegant spa facilities. Here's what you need to know about the Gellért Baths:

Architecture

The Gellért Baths building was constructed between 1912 and 1918, and its design is a prime example of Art Nouveau architecture. The bathhouse's facade features beautiful Zsolnay ceramic tiles and ornate decorations, giving it a striking and elegant appearance.

Indoor Pools

The Gellért Baths offer several indoor thermal pools, each varying in size and temperature. The thermal waters are rich in minerals, believed to have therapeutic benefits for various health conditions.

Outdoor Pool

One of the highlights of the Gellért Baths is its stunning outdoor pool, surrounded by columns, statues, and a beautiful Art Nouveau-style sunbathing terrace. The outdoor pool is open year-round, allowing visitors to enjoy the thermal waters in a unique and picturesque setting.

Steam Rooms and Saunas

The complex includes traditional Turkish steam rooms, Finnish saunas, and aroma cabins, providing visitors with various options for relaxation and rejuvenation.

Massage and Spa Treatments

The Gellért Baths offer a range of spa treatments and massages, allowing visitors to indulge in additional relaxation and pampering.

Art Nouveau Gallery

The bathhouse's main hall features a beautiful Art Nouveau gallery with colorful mosaics and sculptures, adding to the overall charm and elegance of the facility.

Public and Private Baths

The Gellért Baths offer a mix of public and private baths, allowing visitors to choose between shared pools and more secluded, private spaces.

Gellért Hill Location

The Gellért Baths' location at the foot of Gellért Hill offers visitors a serene and scenic environment. After enjoying the baths, visitors can take a short walk up Gellért Hill to admire the panoramic views of Budapest from the Citadella.

St. Stephen's Basilica Architecture

St. Stephen's Basilica, also known as Szent István Bazilika in Hungarian, is a magnificent Roman Catholic basilica located in the heart of Budapest, Hungary. Named in honor of Stephen, the first King of Hungary and the country's patron saint, the basilica is one of the most significant religious and architectural landmarks in the city. Here are some key features of St. Stephen's Basilica's architecture:

Architectural Style

St. Stephen's Basilica is designed in a neoclassical style, influenced by Renaissance and Baroque elements. Its architectural design is the work of Hungarian architect József Hild, who began the construction in 1851. After his death, Miklós Ybl took over the project and completed the basilica in 1905.

Building Plan

The basilica's floor plan is in the shape of a Greek cross, with a central dome and four semicircular apses. This layout is typical of many significant basilicas and emphasizes the centrality of the main altar.

Grand Facade

The front facade of the basilica is adorned with an impressive portico supported by six towering Corinthian columns. Above the entrance, there is a large pediment with a sculptural composition depicting the Holy Trinity.

Dome

The central dome of St. Stephen's Basilica is a dominant feature of its architecture. It reaches a height of 96 meters (315 feet), making it one of the tallest buildings in Budapest. The dome is crowned by a lantern and a cross, visible from various points in the city.

Bell Towers

The basilica has two bell towers flanking the main entrance. The southern tower houses the largest bell in Hungary, weighing approximately 9.5 tons.

Interior Design

The interior of St. Stephen's Basilica is lavishly decorated with frescoes, stuccos, and intricate artwork. The main altar features a beautiful gilded altarpiece dedicated to St. Stephen, while the dome is adorned with mosaic images.

Holy Right Hand Relic

One of the most important religious relics kept in the basilica is the mummified right hand of St. Stephen, which is displayed in a reliquary chapel.

Panoramic View

Visitors can climb a series of stairs or take an elevator to the dome's observation deck, offering stunning panoramic views of Budapest's skyline.

Dohány Street Synagogue

The Dohány Street Synagogue, also known as the Great Synagogue or the Great Synagogue of Budapest, is a magnificent and historically significant Jewish place of worship located in Budapest, Hungary. It is one of the largest synagogues in the world and serves as an essential cultural and religious landmark for Hungary's Jewish community. Here's what you should know about the Dohány Street Synagogue:

Architecture

The Dohány Street Synagogue was designed by the Viennese architect Ludwig Förster and was completed in 1859. Its architectural style is an eclectic mix of Moorish, Romantic, and Byzantine influences, making it a striking and unique building.

Size

The synagogue's grand interior can accommodate up to 3,000 worshipers, while the complex also includes a beautiful courtyard and a Memorial Park dedicated to Holocaust victims.

Exterior

The synagogue's facade features intricate decorations, colorful ceramic tiles, and oriental elements, reflecting the Moorish Revival style prevalent in many synagogues built during the 19th century.

Interior

Inside the synagogue, visitors are treated to a breathtaking sanctuary adorned with elaborate ornamentation, grand chandeliers, and a stunning Ark housing the Torah scrolls.

Jewish Museum

The Dohány Street Synagogue complex includes the Jewish Museum, which exhibits a vast collection of Jewish artifacts, religious objects, and historical items related to Hungary's Jewish heritage.

Heroes' Temple

Adjacent to the main synagogue is the Heroes' Temple, a smaller but equally ornate place of worship dedicated to Jewish soldiers who fought in World War I.

Raoul Wallenberg Memorial Park

The synagogue's courtyard features the Raoul Wallenberg Memorial Park, honoring the Swedish diplomat who saved thousands of Hungarian Jews during the Holocaust.

Jewish Cemetery

The complex includes the Dohány Street Jewish Cemetery, which is one of the oldest and largest Jewish cemeteries in Budapest.

Cultural Events

The Dohány Street Synagogue serves as a cultural and educational center, hosting various events, concerts, and programs that celebrate Jewish culture and heritage.

Great Market Hall (Nagyvásárcsarnok)

The Great Market Hall, known as "Nagyvásárcsarnok" in Hungarian, is one of Budapest's most iconic and bustling marketplaces. Located in the city center, near the Liberty Bridge, this historic market hall is a vibrant hub for locals and tourists alike, offering a wide array of fresh produce, traditional Hungarian products, and a delightful gastronomic experience. Here's what you can expect from the Great Market Hall:

Architecture

The Great Market Hall was designed by Samu Pecz, a renowned Hungarian architect, and it was completed in 1897. The building's architecture features a combination of Gothic, Renaissance, and Art Nouveau elements, creating an impressive and aesthetically pleasing structure.

Interior Layout

The market hall has three levels, with the ground floor primarily dedicated to fresh produce, meats, dairy products, and baked goods. The upper floor houses a variety of souvenir shops, Hungarian crafts, and traditional products, while the basement level features a supermarket and eateries.

Local Products

The market is a treasure trove of Hungarian goods, offering a wide selection of regional specialties, including paprika, Hungarian sausages (kolbász), salami, artisanal cheeses, pickles, and homemade pastries.

Fresh Produce

The market's ground floor is lined with stalls selling fresh fruits, vegetables, herbs, and spices, sourced from local farmers and suppliers.

Gastronomic Delights

The Great Market Hall is an excellent place to sample authentic Hungarian cuisine. Several eateries and food stands offer traditional dishes such as goulash, lángos (deep-fried flatbread), stuffed cabbage, and chimney cake (kürtőskalács).

Souvenirs and Crafts

The upper floor of the market is a treasure trove of souvenirs and traditional Hungarian handicrafts, including embroidered textiles, ceramics, folk costumes, and more.

Culinary Events and Tastings

The Great Market Hall occasionally hosts culinary events, food tastings, and cultural programs that allow visitors to immerse themselves in Hungarian food and traditions.

Local Atmosphere

Visiting the Great Market Hall offers a genuine glimpse into Budapest's local life. It's a place where residents shop for fresh groceries and where tourists can experience authentic Hungarian culture.

Hungarian State Opera House

The Hungarian State Opera House, also known as Magyar Állami Operaház in Hungarian, is a magnificent and prestigious opera house located in the heart of Budapest, Hungary. Designed by the renowned Hungarian architect Miklós Ybl, the opera house is a masterpiece of Neo-Renaissance architecture and a prominent cultural landmark in the city. Here are some key features of the Hungarian State Opera House:

Architecture

The Hungarian State Opera House was constructed between 1875 and 1884, and its architectural style is primarily Neo-Renaissance, with elements of Baroque and Classical influences. Its facade features a grand portico with impressive columns and statues of famous composers.

Interior Grandeur

The interior of the opera house is equally breathtaking, with a lavish and opulent design. The main auditorium is adorned with intricate decorations, gilded ornaments, and stunning frescoes, creating a regal atmosphere for the audience.

Main Auditorium

The main auditorium of the opera house has a seating capacity of approximately 1,300, making it one of the most significant theaters in Hungary. The acoustics are renowned for their exceptional quality, providing an unforgettable experience for opera and ballet performances.

Royal Box

The opera house includes a Royal Box, which was once reserved for the Habsburg Emperor and other dignitaries. Today, it is used for special guests and distinguished visitors.

Chandelier

The main chandelier in the auditorium is an exquisite piece of craftsmanship, adding to the grandeur and elegance of the interior.

Cultural Events

The Hungarian State Opera House hosts a diverse program of opera, ballet, classical music concerts, and other cultural performances throughout the year. It is home to the Hungarian National Ballet and the Hungarian State Opera.

Guided Tours

Visitors can take guided tours of the opera house, providing a behind-the-scenes look at the building's history, architecture, and backstage areas.

Importance in Hungarian Culture

The Hungarian State Opera House is not only an architectural gem but also a symbol of Hungary's rich cultural heritage. It has played a vital role in promoting the arts and nurturing talented artists for more than a century.

Vajdahunyad Castle Architecture

Vajdahunyad Castle, also known as Vajdahunyad vára in Hungarian, is a stunning and eclectic castle located in Budapest, Hungary. Situated in the City Park (Városliget), the castle is a popular tourist attraction and a unique architectural ensemble that showcases various historical styles and Hungarian landmarks. Here are some key features of Vajdahunyad Castle:

Architecture

Vajdahunyad Castle was originally built in 1896 as part of the Millennial Exhibition, celebrating the 1,000th anniversary of the Hungarian conquest. The castle's design is an eclectic mix of architectural styles, representing various Hungarian historical buildings.

Inspiration

The castle's architectural elements draw inspiration from different periods and regions of Hungary, including Romanesque, Gothic, Renaissance, and Baroque styles. Its design is reminiscent of famous Hungarian landmarks, such as the Hunyad Castle in Transylvania (now in Romania).

Composition

Vajdahunyad Castle consists of several sections, each representing a different historical building style. The structure includes a mix of towers, turrets, and facades, making it a fascinating and visually captivating ensemble.

Transylvanian Wing

The most iconic part of the castle is the Transylvanian Wing, which closely resembles the Hunyad Castle in Transylvania. The wing features a drawbridge, Gothic-style windows, and other architectural details typical of medieval castles.

Agricultural Museum

One section of the castle houses the Hungarian Agricultural Museum (Magyar Mezőgazdasági Múzeum), which showcases Hungary's agricultural history and rural traditions.

Seasonal Events

Throughout the year, Vajdahunyad Castle hosts various cultural events, festivals, and exhibitions, making it a lively and vibrant cultural hub within Budapest.

Surroundings

The castle is surrounded by a scenic artificial lake, providing a picturesque setting that enhances its charm and allure.

Photo Spot

Vajdahunyad Castle is a favorite spot for photographers and visitors seeking to capture its unique architecture and picturesque backdrop.

Budapest Palace of Arts (Müpa Budapest)

The Budapest Palace of Arts, also known as Müpa Budapest, is a prominent cultural and arts complex located on the Danube Promenade in Budapest, Hungary. Müpa Budapest serves as a major cultural hub in the city, hosting a wide range of artistic performances, including concerts, theater productions, dance shows, and visual arts exhibitions. Here are some key features of the Budapest Palace of Arts (Müpa Budapest):

Architecture

Müpa Budapest was designed by the renowned Hungarian architect Zoboky, Demeter and Partners, and it was opened to the public in 2005. The building's design is a contemporary masterpiece, combining modern architectural elements with a sleek and minimalist aesthetic.

Venue Spaces

The complex includes multiple performance venues, including the Béla Bartók National Concert Hall, the Festival Theater, and the Ludwig Museum of Contemporary Art.

Béla Bartók National Concert Hall

The concert hall is the centerpiece of Müpa Budapest, known for its exceptional acoustics and world-class facilities. It hosts classical music concerts, orchestral performances, and other musical events.

Festival Theater

The theater is a versatile space that can accommodate various performances, such as theater plays, dance shows, and opera productions.

Ludwig Museum of Contemporary Art

The Ludwig Museum is dedicated to contemporary and modern art, featuring an impressive collection of Hungarian and international artworks.

Program Diversity

Müpa Budapest offers a diverse and extensive program, ranging from classical and contemporary music concerts to ballet, opera, jazz, world music, and theater performances.

Hungarian and International Artists

The complex hosts performances by both Hungarian and international artists, attracting talent from all over the world.

Educational and Cultural Programs

In addition to its regular performances, Müpa Budapest also offers educational programs, workshops, and cultural events, engaging with the local community and promoting arts education.

Riverfront Location

Müpa Budapest's location along the Danube River provides a scenic backdrop for visitors and offers stunning views of Budapest's iconic landmarks, such as the Hungarian Parliament Building and Buda Castle.

Architecture and Design Awards

Müpa Budapest has received numerous awards and accolades for its architectural design and contributions to the cultural scene in Budapest.

The Innovative Whale (Bálna Budapest)

The Whale, also known as "Bálna Budapest" in Hungarian, is a unique and innovative building located along the Danube River in Budapest, Hungary. Designed by Dutch architect Kas Oosterhuis, the Whale is a contemporary cultural and commercial complex that has become a significant addition to Budapest's urban landscape. Here are some key features of the Whale (Bálna Budapest):

Architecture

The Whale's design is characterized by its striking and unconventional appearance. The building's exterior resembles the shape of a whale, which inspired its name. The glass facade and curvilinear structure contribute to its modern and futuristic look.

Location

The Whale is situated on the Pest side of the Danube River, near the Liberty Bridge, providing a picturesque waterfront setting.

Multifunctional Complex

The building serves as a multifunctional cultural and commercial complex, accommodating various activities and amenities under one roof.

Cultural and Event Spaces

The Whale houses exhibition halls, event spaces, and galleries, making it an ideal venue for hosting cultural events, art exhibitions, and performances.

Retail and Dining

The complex includes shops, boutiques, and restaurants, offering visitors a diverse range of retail and dining experiences.

Entertainment and Leisure

The Whale provides leisure and entertainment options, such as cafes and bars, where visitors can relax and enjoy the scenic views of the Danube River.

Public Spaces

The building's interior and exterior spaces are designed to provide inviting public areas, creating a lively and vibrant atmosphere.

Sustainable Design

The Whale incorporates sustainable design features, such as energy-efficient systems and materials, in line with modern architectural practices.

Integration with the Urban Environment

The Whale's unique design and waterfront location have made it a notable landmark that complements the surrounding urban environment.

Visitor Attraction

The Whale has quickly become a popular destination for both locals and tourists, attracting visitors with its eye-catching architecture and diverse offerings.

MONUMENTS AND STATUES

Budapest is adorned with numerous statues and sculptures, each contributing to the city's rich cultural heritage and historical significance. These statues are scattered throughout the city, gracing public squares, parks, and prominent landmarks. Here are some notable statues in Budapest:

Imre Nagy Memorial

The Imre Nagy Memorial is a significant monument in Budapest, Hungary, dedicated to the memory of Imre Nagy, a prominent political figure who played a crucial role during the Hungarian Revolution of 1956. The memorial commemorates his life and legacy as a symbol of resistance and courage in the face of Soviet oppression. Here are some key details about the Imre Nagy Memorial:

Location

The Imre Nagy Memorial is located in Martyrs' Square (Mártírok tér) in Budapest, near the Hungarian Parliament Building.

Imre Nagy

Imre Nagy was a Hungarian communist politician who initially served as Prime Minister of Hungary during the 1953-1955 period and then again during the 1956 Hungarian Revolution. He was known for advocating reforms and seeking to steer Hungary towards a more independent path within the Soviet bloc.

Role in the 1956 Hungarian Revolution

During the Hungarian Revolution of 1956, Imre Nagy emerged as a symbol of the uprising's democratic ideals and aspirations for freedom from Soviet control. He declared Hungary's withdrawal from the Warsaw Pact and called for democratic reforms.

Betrayal and Execution

The Soviet Union's response to the Hungarian Revolution was swift and brutal. Imre Nagy was arrested by Soviet forces in 1956 and later tried in a secret trial. He was charged with treason and sentenced to death. On June 16, 1958, he was executed by hanging.

Unmarked Grave

After his execution, Imre Nagy's body was buried in an unmarked grave within a prison courtyard, and his name became taboo during the years of Soviet rule.

Memorial Construction

Following the fall of communism in Hungary in 1989, efforts were made to honor the memory of Imre Nagy and his fellow martyrs. The Imre Nagy Memorial was built in Martyrs' Square in 1996, marking the 40th anniversary of the Hungarian Revolution.

Monument Design

The memorial features a 1956-style Hungarian flag flying atop a tall pole. It is surrounded by bronze statues of the martyrs of the revolution, including Imre Nagy. The memorial is a somber and powerful tribute to those who fought for freedom and democracy during the revolution.

Steve Jobs Memorial Statue

After Steve Jobs passed away on October 5, 2011, people from around the world expressed their condolences and paid tribute to the co-founder of Apple. In the wake of his death, a Hungarian software company decided to honor his memory with a statue. This heartfelt gesture resulted in the world's first memorial statue of Steve Jobs.

The statue was revealed on December 21, 2011, at Graphisoft Park, a science and technology park established by Graphisoft in 1997. The commission came from Gabor Bojar, the founder and chairman of Graphisoft, a software company that caught Jobs' attention in the 1980s.

Their connection began when Bojar and Jobs met at an information technology trade show in Germany in 1984. Graphisoft was showcasing its ArchiCAD three-dimensional design software, and Jobs was deeply impressed. He decided to support the small Hungarian company, which was operating in the constraints of communist Hungary. Apple provided financial assistance, computers, and introduced Graphisoft to its global distribution network, forever changing the fate of the Hungarian startup.

When Bojar learned about Jobs' passing, he felt compelled to create a fitting tribute. He enlisted the talent of Hungarian sculptor Erno Toth, who quickly got to work sculpting a life-size bronze statue of Jobs. Toth completed the statue in less than two months, and it was unveiled outside the Graphisoft headquarters.

The realistic statue portrays Jobs in his signature attire: a long-sleeved mock turtleneck, Levi's 501 jeans, sneakers, and round glasses. The pose captures Jobs in his iconic on-stage role, presenting with passion and enthusiasm. One arm is raised in a gesture of explanation, while the other holds a remote control used during his captivating presentations.

Located near the statue's feet is a simple memorial plaque bearing one of Jobs' most famous quotes: "The only way to do great work is to love what you do." The plaque itself is thoughtfully shaped like an iPad, a nod to the revolutionary products that Jobs helped create.

The Steve Jobs Memorial Statue can be found outside the Graphisoft headquarters in Graphisoft Park. The park houses several high-tech companies, including Microsoft, SAP, Servier, Canon, and more, making it a center of innovation and technology in Budapest, Hungary. To visit the memorial, head to Záhony utca 7, which is situated north of the city center.

Army Statues

During the communist era, Hungary was under the influence of the Soviet Union, and as a result, various statues and images related to the army and communist ideology were prominent in public spaces. After the fall of communism in 1989, many of these statues were removed, relocated, or transformed to reflect Hungary's new democratic identity. Some significant army and communist-related statues and images included:

Red Army Soldier Statues

During the communist era, statues of Red Army soldiers were prevalent in public squares, symbolizing the presence of Soviet forces in Hungary.

Soviet Liberation Monument

The Soviet Liberation Monument, also known as the Monument to Soviet Heroes, was erected to commemorate the Red Army's role in liberating Hungary from Nazi occupation during World War II. It featured a towering obelisk and sculptural elements.

Lenin Statues

Statues of Vladimir Lenin, the leader of the Russian Revolution and an influential figure in communist ideology, were widespread across Hungary during the communist era.

Karl Marx Statue

As one of the founders of communist theory, statues of Karl Marx were also found in various cities and towns in Hungary.

Heroes' Square (Hősök tere)

Before the fall of communism, Heroes' Square in Budapest featured statues of historical figures and socialist leaders, including statues of communist leaders such as Béla Kun and Mátyás Rákosi.

Socialist Realism Art

Communist propaganda often used art in the form of murals and posters to promote socialist values and ideology, glorifying the working class and socialist achievements.

The Statue of Liberty (Szabadság Szobor)

The Statue of Liberty, known as "Szabadság Szobor" in Hungarian, is one of the most iconic and significant statues in Budapest, Hungary. It stands on top of Gellért Hill, offering breathtaking views of the city and the Danube River. Here are some key features and historical background of the Statue of Liberty:

Commemoration of Liberation

The Statue of Liberty was erected in 1947 as a symbol of Hungary's liberation from Nazi occupation during World War II. It commemorates the Soviet Red Army's role in driving out the German forces and liberating Budapest.

Design and Architecture

The statue was designed by Hungarian sculptor Zsigmond Kisfaludi Strobl and stands at a height of approximately 14 meters (46 feet). The figure of a woman holding a palm leaf aloft represents liberty and victory.

Female Allegorical Figure

The Statue of Liberty's design is reminiscent of an allegorical female figure commonly found in many liberty statues worldwide. She is portrayed with a raised palm leaf, symbolizing peace and freedom.

Location

The statue is strategically positioned on Gellért Hill, providing a commanding view of Budapest and becoming a significant landmark visible from various points in the city.

Controversial History

During Hungary's communist era, the Statue of Liberty became a symbol of the Soviet Union's influence over the country. It was often used in propaganda and was considered a representation of the communist regime. As a result, it became a contentious issue after the fall of communism.

Changes after 1989

Following the collapse of communism in 1989, the inscription "To the memory of the liberating Soviet heroes" was removed from the base of the statue. It has since been rededicated as a monument to all those who sacrificed their lives for Hungary's independence and freedom.

Attraction for Visitors

The Statue of Liberty remains a popular tourist attraction, with visitors making their way up Gellért Hill to appreciate the views and pay homage to Hungary's historical struggles for freedom.

Shoes on the Danube Bank

The Shoes on the Danube Bank is a powerful and moving memorial located on the banks of the Danube River in Budapest, Hungary. The memorial serves as a poignant reminder of the tragic events that occurred during World War II, specifically the Holocaust and the loss of countless lives. Here are some key details about the Shoes on the Danube Bank:

Historical Background

The Shoes on the Danube Bank memorial was created in 2005 to commemorate the Jews who were victims of the Arrow Cross militia, a fascist organization in Hungary, during the final years of World War II.

Design and Concept

The memorial consists of sixty pairs of iron shoes, representing the footwear that Jewish men, women, and children were forced to remove before being shot at the edge of the Danube River. The victims were then left to fall into the river, where their bodies were carried away by the current.

Location

The Shoes on the Danube Bank is located on the Pest side of the river, close to the Hungarian Parliament Building. It is easily accessible and serves as a somber reminder of the atrocities that took place during the Holocaust.

Symbolism

The shoes represent the empty spaces left by those who lost their lives during the horrific events of the Holocaust. They symbolize the absence of the victims and serve as a powerful testament to the human tragedy and loss experienced during that time.

Impact

The memorial has a profound emotional impact on visitors, prompting reflection on the horrors of war and the importance of remembering the victims of the Holocaust.

Public Commemoration

The Shoes on the Danube Bank is a public space where people can pay their respects, leave flowers, or light candles in memory of the victims. It has become a place of remembrance and a symbol of hope for a more tolerant and compassionate world.

Matthias Fountain (Mátyás Kútja)

The Matthias Fountain, known as "Mátyás Kútja" in Hungarian, is an exquisite neo-Baroque fountain located in front of the Buda Castle in Budapest, Hungary. It is one of the most beautiful and famous fountains in the city, attracting both locals and tourists with its intricate design and historical significance. Here are some key details about the Matthias Fountain:

Historical Background

The fountain was constructed in 1904 on the occasion of the millennium celebration of Hungary. It was designed by Alajos Stróbl, a renowned Hungarian sculptor, as part of the efforts to beautify the Buda Castle area.

Location

The Matthias Fountain is strategically positioned in Trinity Square (Szentháromság tér), a central square in front of the Buda Castle, which is a UNESCO World Heritage Site.

Design and Features

The fountain is a grandiose work of art, featuring a central column adorned with a statue of King Matthias Corvinus, one of Hungary's most illustrious medieval rulers. King Matthias is depicted in royal regalia, sitting on a throne and holding a scepter and orb, symbolizing his authority.

Lions and Hunyadi Coat of Arms

Surrounding the central column, there are four bronze lions, each holding a shield displaying the coat of arms of the influential Hunyadi family. The Hunyadi family played a significant role in Hungarian history, and King Matthias was a member of this esteemed dynasty.

Triton Figures

At the base of the fountain, there are Triton figures blowing conch shells, adding to the artistic splendor of the monument. The Tritons represent water deities from Greek mythology.

Renovations

Over the years, the Matthias Fountain has undergone several renovations to restore its original beauty and preserve its historical value. These efforts have ensured that the fountain remains a stunning attraction for visitors to enjoy.

Symbolic Meaning

The Matthias Fountain is not only an exquisite piece of art but also holds symbolic significance for Hungary. It pays tribute to King Matthias Corvinus, a beloved ruler known for his fair and just rule during the Hungarian Renaissance.

Anonymous Statue (Ismeretlen Írók Tere)

The Anonymous Statue, known as "Ismeretlen Írók Tere" in Hungarian, is a captivating and thought-provoking sculpture located in Budapest, Hungary. The statue holds great significance as it represents all unknown writers and serves as a tribute to the countless anonymous authors whose contributions to literature and creativity remain unrecognized. Here are some key details about the Anonymous Statue:

Location

The Anonymous Statue is situated in Ismeretlen Írók Tere, which translates to "Unknown Writers' Square," located near the famous Fisherman's Bastion and Matthias Church in the Buda Castle District.

Design and Sculptor

The statue was created by sculptor László Marton in 1903. It is a bronze statue depicting a cloaked, seated figure holding a quill and parchment, symbolizing a writer in anonymity.

Symbolism

The primary symbolism of the Anonymous Statue lies in its representation of the countless writers and poets whose identities remain unknown to history. The figure embodies the collective creative spirit, acknowledging the contributions of all those whose names have been lost to time.

Literature and Creativity

The statue serves as a reminder of the power of literature and creative expression. It pays tribute to the writers and poets who, despite their anonymity, have left a lasting impact on Hungarian culture and literature.

Historic Setting

The Anonymous Statue is surrounded by historical landmarks, creating a charming and evocative atmosphere that adds to its appeal as a cultural monument.

Celebrating the Anonymous

By celebrating unknown writers, the statue highlights the universal struggles and triumphs of creative minds throughout history. It invites visitors to contemplate the significance of artistic expression and the enduring power of words.

Little Princess (Kiskirálylány)

The Little Princess, known as "Kiskirálylány" in Hungarian, is a beloved and enchanting statue located in Budapest, Hungary. Situated near the Danube Promenade, the statue is a charming depiction of a young girl peering over the railing of the city's waterfront. Here are some key details about the Little Princess statue:

Location

The Little Princess statue is located on the Pest side of Budapest, specifically on the Danube Promenade (Duna korzó), near the famous Chain Bridge.

Sculptor

The statue was created by Hungarian sculptor László Marton and was unveiled in 1972 as a part of the "Little Princess" poem and statue series.

Design and Features

The Little Princess statue portrays a young girl in a flowing dress, sitting on the edge of the promenade's railing with her feet dangling over the Danube River. She is looking wistfully towards the Buda side of the city.

Inspired by a Poem

The Little Princess statue was inspired by a poem written by Hungarian poet Mihály Vörösmarty. The poem, titled "The Little Princess," is a romantic and melancholic work that captures the spirit of Budapest and the Danube.

Popularity and Symbolism

The statue has become an endearing symbol of Budapest, evoking a sense of nostalgia and innocence. It is loved by both locals and visitors alike and has become a popular spot for taking photographs and enjoying scenic views of the river and Buda Castle.

Renovations

Over the years, the Little Princess statue has undergone maintenance and renovations to preserve its original charm and artistic beauty.

Adjacent to the Chain Bridge

The statue's location near the Chain Bridge makes it a prominent landmark that is easily accessible to tourists exploring Budapest's city center.

Ronald Reagan Statue

The Ronald Reagan Statue in Budapest, Hungary, is a significant monument dedicated to the 40th President of the United States, Ronald Reagan. The statue commemorates Reagan's role in promoting freedom and democracy, particularly during the final years of the Cold War. Here are some key details about the Ronald Reagan Statue:

Location

The statue is located near the Hungarian Parliament Building in Liberty Square (Szabadság tér) in Budapest.

Commemoration

The Ronald Reagan Statue was unveiled on June 29, 2011, to honor the former U.S. President's contributions to the cause of freedom and democracy around the world.

Symbolism

The statue serves as a symbol of the strong ties between Hungary and the United States and commemorates Ronald Reagan's role in advocating for human rights and supporting countries seeking to break free from communist oppression.

Role in Ending the Cold War

Ronald Reagan played a significant role in the eventual collapse of the Soviet Union and the end of the Cold War. His policies and speeches, particularly his famous "Tear Down This Wall" speech in Berlin in 1987, challenged the Eastern Bloc's communist regimes and encouraged democratic reforms.

Sculptor

The bronze statue of Ronald Reagan was created by Hungarian sculptor István Zsófi and is depicted in a standing pose, capturing his characteristic warmth and determination.

Public Opinion

The unveiling of the Ronald Reagan Statue was met with both support and criticism. Supporters viewed it as a tribute to a leader who championed freedom and democracy, while critics argued that it symbolized Hungary's alignment with U.S. policies during the Cold War era.

Historical Significance

The statue serves as a reminder of the complex historical and political relations between Hungary and the United States during the Cold War period.

Ferenc Liszt Monument

The Ferenc Liszt Monument is a significant statue dedicated to the renowned Hungarian composer and pianist, Franz Liszt, also known as Ferenc Liszt in Hungarian. As one of Hungary's most celebrated cultural figures, Liszt's musical contributions and legacy are commemorated through this impressive monument. Here are some key details about the Ferenc Liszt Monument:

Location

The Ferenc Liszt Monument is located in Budapest, Hungary's capital city. It can be found in front of the Academy of Music (Liszt Ferenc

Zeneművészeti Egyetem), a fitting location as Liszt was an influential music educator and founded the Academy.

Unveiling

The statue was unveiled in 1906, on the centenary of Liszt's birth, to honor his memory and recognize his immense contributions to the world of music.

Design and Sculptor

The statue was designed by renowned Hungarian sculptor Alajos Stróbl. It features a larger-than-life bronze statue of Franz Liszt in a standing pose. Liszt is depicted holding a sheet of music, reflecting his status as a composer and conductor.

Symbolism

The monument is not only a tribute to Ferenc Liszt but also symbolizes Hungary's appreciation for its rich musical heritage and cultural contributions.

Cultural Legacy

Franz Liszt was a prolific composer and virtuoso pianist during the Romantic era. He was known for his innovative compositions, virtuosic piano performances, and his contributions to the development of modern music. The monument pays homage to his enduring influence on classical music.

Influence on Music Education

In addition to his artistic achievements, Liszt also played a vital role in music education. He established the Academy of Music in Budapest, which became a prestigious institution nurturing generations of talented musicians.

Attraction for Music Lovers

The Ferenc Liszt Monument is not only an important cultural symbol for Hungary but also a popular destination for music lovers and tourists seeking to pay tribute to one of the greatest composers and pianists in history.

BUDAPEST MARKETS

Hold Street Market Hall (Hold utcai Piac)

Hold Street Market Hall, also known as Hold utcai Piac in Hungarian, is a charming market located near Andrassy Avenue in Budapest, Hungary. It is a popular destination for locals and visitors seeking fresh produce, local specialties, and an authentic market experience. Here's more information about Hold Street Market Hall:

Location and Atmosphere

Hold Street Market Hall is situated in the heart of Budapest, near Nyugati Railway Station and within walking distance of popular attractions like Andrassy Avenue and Heroes' Square. The market hall itself is housed in a beautiful historic building and exudes a cozy and bustling atmosphere.

Fresh Produce

The market is renowned for its wide variety of fresh fruits, vegetables, herbs, and spices. Local farmers and vendors offer an array of seasonal produce, allowing visitors to experience the flavors and ingredients that are key to Hungarian cuisine. The quality and freshness of the products make it a favorite spot for grocery shopping among locals.

Traditional Hungarian Delicacies

Hold Street Market Hall is a great place to sample traditional Hungarian delicacies. Numerous stalls offer local specialties like sausages, cured meats, cheeses, pickles, and pastries. Don't miss the opportunity to try Hungarian lángos, a deep-fried dough topped with various savory or sweet toppings.

Butchers and Fishmongers

The market is home to several butchers and fishmongers who offer a wide range of high-quality meats, poultry, and fresh fish. You can find a variety of cuts, including popular Hungarian specialties like Mangalica pork. The fishmongers provide a selection of locally caught freshwater fish.

Bakeries and Pastries

Hold Street Market Hall features a selection of bakeries and pastry stalls, enticing visitors with delicious bread, pastries, and sweet treats. It's an excellent place to try traditional Hungarian pastries like chimney cake (kürtőskalács), strudel, and pogácsa (savory scones).

Local Products and Specialty Stores

The market also houses specialty stores selling a range of Hungarian products, such as spices, honey, paprika, Hungarian wines, and handmade crafts. These stores offer unique and authentic items that make for great souvenirs or gifts.

Street Food Stalls

Outside the market hall, you'll find street food stalls offering a variety of quick bites and snacks. This is an opportunity to try local street food favorites like lángos, sausage sandwiches, and chimney cakes, which can be enjoyed on the go.

Great Market Hall

The Great Market Hall, also known as Central Market Hall or Nagyvásárcsarnok in Hungarian, is a bustling and iconic market located in the heart of Budapest. It is the largest and oldest indoor market in the city, offering a wide variety of fresh produce, local delicacies, and traditional Hungarian products. Here's more information about the Great Market Hall:

History and Architecture

The Great Market Hall was built in 1897 and designed by renowned Hungarian architect Samu Pecz. The building features an impressive facade with ornate ironwork and colorful Zsolnay ceramic roof tiles. Its architectural style is a blend of Gothic, Renaissance, and Art Nouveau influences.

Market Hall Layout

The market is divided into three levels. The ground floor is dedicated to fresh produce, including fruits, vegetables, meat, fish, and dairy products. The upper floor offers a variety of stalls selling Hungarian souvenirs, handicrafts, clothing, spices, sweets, and more. The basement level houses a supermarket, wine shops, and eateries.

Hungarian Cuisine

The Great Market Hall is an excellent place to sample traditional Hungarian cuisine. Numerous stalls and eateries offer local dishes such as goulash, lángos (deep-fried flatbread), chimney cake (kürtőskalács), sausages, pickles, and Hungarian pastries like strudel and dobos torte. It's a great opportunity to taste the flavors of Hungary and experience its culinary culture.

Local Products and Souvenirs

The market is a treasure trove of Hungarian products and souvenirs. You can find a wide range of items including paprika, Hungarian wines, honey, embroidery, pottery, leather goods, and more. It's a perfect place to pick up authentic and unique gifts to take home.

Market Atmosphere

The Great Market Hall offers a vibrant and lively atmosphere. It's a hub of activity with locals shopping for their daily groceries and tourists exploring the stalls. The market buzzes with energy, colors, aromas, and the sounds of vendors engaging with customers.

Events and Culinary Workshops

The Great Market Hall occasionally hosts special events, culinary workshops, and food festivals. These events showcase the diversity of Hungarian cuisine and provide opportunities to learn about traditional cooking techniques and ingredients.

Photography Opportunities

The architectural beauty and vibrant scenes inside the Great Market Hall make it a popular spot for photography enthusiasts. The colorful displays of fruits, vegetables, and Hungarian products, along with the lively interactions between vendors and customers, create memorable photo opportunities.

Lehel Market (Lehel tér)

Lehel Market, located in Lehel tér in Budapest, Hungary, is a bustling open-air market that offers a wide range of fresh produce, local specialties, and everyday goods. It is a popular shopping destination for locals and visitors alike. Here's more information about Lehel Market:

Location and Accessibility

Lehel Market is situated in the Újlipótváros neighborhood, near the Nyugati Railway Station and Margaret Bridge. Its central location makes it easily accessible by public transportation, including tram lines and the metro.

Fresh Produce

The market is known for its abundant selection of fresh fruits, vegetables, herbs, and spices. Local farmers and vendors offer a diverse array of seasonal produce, ensuring a vibrant and colorful market experience. The quality and variety of the produce attract both locals looking for fresh ingredients and visitors seeking an authentic market atmosphere.

Meat, Fish, and Dairy Products

Lehel Market features stalls selling a range of high-quality meats, including beef, pork, poultry, and sausages. Fishmongers offer a selection of fresh fish, including local varieties from Hungary's freshwater rivers and lakes. The market is also home to vendors selling dairy products like cheese, butter, and yogurt.

Hungarian Delicacies and Street Food

The market offers an opportunity to savor traditional Hungarian delicacies. You can find stalls selling local specialties such as lángos (deep-fried flatbread), goulash, stuffed cabbage, and various types of pastries. These treats are perfect for a quick bite while exploring the market.

Bakery and Pastry Stalls

Lehel Market hosts several bakeries and pastry stalls where you can find freshly baked bread, rolls, pastries, and cakes. The aroma of freshly baked goods fills the air, inviting you to try Hungarian delights like strudel, pogácsa (savory scones), and sweet pastries.

Household Goods and Non-Food Items

In addition to food items, Lehel Market offers a range of everyday household goods and non-food items. You can find items such as kitchenware, clothing, accessories, flowers, plants, and more.

Local Market Experience

Lehel Market provides an authentic local market experience. It is a place where Budapest residents shop for their daily groceries and socialize with vendors and neighbors. Engaging with the friendly vendors and experiencing the lively atmosphere gives you a taste of everyday life in Budapest.

Ecseri Flea Market (Ecseri Piac)

The Ecseri Flea Market, known as Ecseri Piac in Hungarian, is a renowned open-air market located on the outskirts of Budapest. It is a treasure trove for antique lovers, collectors, and those seeking unique finds. Here's more information about the Ecseri Flea Market:

Location and Access

The Ecseri Flea Market is situated in the 19th district of Budapest, approximately 10 kilometers southeast of the city center. While it may be a bit outside the central areas, it is easily accessible by public transportation, including bus and tram lines.

Antique and Vintage Goods

The market specializes in selling a wide range of antique and vintage items, making it a paradise for collectors and enthusiasts. You can find an impressive assortment of items such as antique furniture, vintage clothing, ceramics, glassware, silverware, artwork, books, coins, jewelry, clocks, and much more. The market's diverse offerings cater to various tastes and interests.

Authentic Hungarian Collectibles

Ecseri Flea Market is an excellent place to find authentic Hungarian collectibles and traditional handicrafts. You can discover unique items that reflect Hungary's rich cultural heritage, including folk art, embroidered textiles, traditional costumes, and other ethnographic treasures.

Bargaining and Negotiating

Bargaining is an essential part of the market experience, and it is expected at Ecseri Flea Market. Negotiating with the vendors can be an enjoyable and interactive process. However, it's always important to be respectful and fair while haggling over prices.

Knowledgeable Vendors

The market's vendors are often well-informed about the history and background of the items they sell. They can provide insights, stories, and details about the antiques and collectibles, adding an extra layer of fascination to the shopping experience.

Food and Refreshments

Ecseri Flea Market offers several food stalls and snack bars where you can take a break from shopping and enjoy a meal or refreshments. These spots typically serve Hungarian street food and traditional snacks, allowing you to refuel and continue exploring the market.

Hidden Gems and Unique Finds

With its vast array of items and ever-changing inventory, the Ecseri Flea Market is full of hidden gems and unexpected treasures waiting to be discovered. Exploring the stalls and browsing through the various stands is an adventure in itself, and you never know what hidden gem you might stumble upon.

Fény Street Market (Fény utcai Piac)

Fény Street Market, or Fény utcai Piac in Hungarian, is a local market in Budapest that offers a variety of fresh produce, specialty food items, and everyday essentials. Located in the Újlipótváros neighborhood, it provides a convenient shopping experience for locals and visitors alike. Here's more information about Fény Street Market:

Location and Accessibility

Fény Street Market is situated in the 13th district of Budapest, near Margaret Island and the Danube River. It is easily accessible by public transportation, including tram lines and bus routes. The market's central location makes it a convenient stop for locals and tourists in the area.

Fresh Produce

The market is known for its wide selection of fresh fruits, vegetables, herbs, and spices. Local farmers and vendors offer a range of seasonal produce, allowing visitors to enjoy the flavors and quality of locally grown ingredients. From ripe tomatoes and colorful peppers to aromatic herbs, you'll find a variety of options to choose from.

Meat, Dairy, and Bakery Products

Fény Street Market features stalls offering a range of meat, poultry, and dairy products. You can find high-quality cuts of beef, pork, chicken, and other meats, as well as a variety of cheeses, yogurt, butter, and other dairy items. The market also hosts bakeries that offer freshly baked bread, pastries, and cakes.

Hungarian Specialties

The market is a great place to explore and sample traditional Hungarian specialties. You'll find local products like paprika, Hungarian sausages, pickles, honey, jams, and other artisanal food items. These specialties showcase the unique flavors and culinary heritage of Hungary.

Flowers and Plants

Fény Street Market includes stalls selling a colorful array of flowers and plants. From vibrant bouquets to potted plants, you can find a selection of flora to brighten your home or to offer as a thoughtful gift.

Household and Non-Food Items

In addition to food products, Fény Street Market offers a range of household goods and non-food items. You'll find vendors selling kitchenware, cleaning supplies, textiles, clothing, accessories, and more. It's a convenient one-stop-shop for everyday necessities.

Local Market Experience

Fény Street Market provides an authentic local market experience, with a friendly and welcoming atmosphere. It is a place where residents of the Újlipótváros neighborhood shop for their daily groceries and interact with vendors. Engaging with the local community and exploring the market offers a glimpse into the daily life of Budapest residents.

BUDAPEST MUSEUMS

Hungarian National Museum

The Hungarian National Museum, known as Magyar Nemzeti Múzeum in Hungarian, is a prominent museum located in Budapest, Hungary. It is one of the most important cultural institutions in the country and is dedicated to preserving and showcasing Hungary's history, culture, and art. Here's more information about the Hungarian National Museum:

History

The Hungarian National Museum was founded in 1802 and is one of the oldest national museums in Europe. Its establishment aimed to collect and preserve Hungarian historical artifacts and promote national identity and cultural heritage.

Building and Architecture

The museum is housed in an impressive neoclassical building located in the Pest district of Budapest. Designed by architect Mihály Pollack, the building itself is considered a masterpiece of Hungarian architecture. Its grand façade and imposing colonnade make it a significant landmark in the city.

Collections

The Hungarian National Museum boasts a vast collection that spans various periods and topics related to Hungarian history and culture. The museum's permanent exhibitions cover areas such as archaeology, numismatics, medieval art, ethnography, and Hungarian history from ancient times to the present day.

Highlights

Among the notable artifacts and displays in the museum, some highlights include the Coronation Mantle and Crown Jewels, which represent the country's royal history. The medieval stone carvings, including the famous Árpád Dynasty sculptures, are also important attractions. The museum also houses a collection of Hungarian fine arts and significant historical documents.

Temporary Exhibitions

In addition to its permanent collections, the Hungarian National Museum hosts temporary exhibitions that explore various aspects of Hungarian culture, history, and art. These exhibitions provide additional insights into specific topics and offer visitors a chance to explore different aspects of Hungarian heritage.

Educational Programs and Events

The museum offers educational programs, guided tours, and workshops for both children and adults. These programs aim to engage visitors with interactive and informative experiences, allowing them to delve deeper into the history and culture of Hungary.

Research and Library

The Hungarian National Museum has an extensive research library that serves as a resource for scholars, researchers, and students. The library houses a vast collection of books, periodicals, and archival materials related to Hungarian history and culture.

Museum of Fine Arts

The Museum of Fine Arts, known as Szépművészeti Múzeum in Hungarian, is one of Budapest's premier art museums. It houses a vast collection of artworks from various periods and styles, including European paintings, sculptures, and applied arts. Here's more information about the Museum of Fine Arts:

History

The Museum of Fine Arts was established in 1896 and opened its doors to the public in 1906. The museum was built to commemorate the thousandth anniversary of the founding of Hungary. Its purpose was to showcase the nation's cultural wealth and promote art appreciation.

Building and Architecture

The museum's building is an architectural gem in itself. Designed by architects Albert Schickedanz and Fülöp Herzog, it features an impressive Neoclassical design with a grand entrance and a monumental dome. The exterior of the building is adorned with sculptures and decorative elements.

Collections

The Museum of Fine Arts houses a diverse collection of artworks from various periods, ranging from ancient Egyptian and Classical art to European paintings and sculptures from the Middle Ages to the 20th century. The collection includes masterpieces by renowned artists such as Rembrandt, Raphael, El Greco, Velázquez, Monet, and many others.

European Paintings

The museum's European painting collection is particularly noteworthy. It encompasses works from the Italian Renaissance, Baroque, and Romantic periods, as well as pieces from the Dutch Golden Age, French Impressionism, and Post-Impressionism. Visitors can admire iconic paintings like Titian's "Venus with a Mirror" and Bruegel's "The Wedding Dance."

Sculpture Collection

The Museum of Fine Arts has an extensive sculpture collection, featuring works from ancient Greece, Rome, and Egypt, as well as European sculptures from the Middle Ages to the modern era. The collection includes notable pieces like Rodin's "The Age of Bronze" and Michelangelo's "Madonna and Child."

Applied Arts

In addition to paintings and sculptures, the museum houses a significant collection of applied arts. Visitors can explore exquisite examples of decorative arts, including ceramics, textiles, furniture, and metalwork, showcasing different periods and styles.

Temporary Exhibitions and Events

The Museum of Fine Arts hosts temporary exhibitions that cover various art-related topics and themes. These exhibitions provide an opportunity to see additional artworks and delve deeper into specific areas of art history. The museum also organizes lectures, concerts, and other cultural events.

Hungarian National Gallery

The Hungarian National Gallery, known as Magyar Nemzeti Galéria in Hungarian, is a prominent art museum located in Buda Castle in Budapest, Hungary. It is dedicated to collecting, preserving, and exhibiting Hungarian art from the medieval period to the present day. Here's more information about the Hungarian National Gallery:

History

The Hungarian National Gallery was established in 1957 as a separate institution from the Hungarian National Museum, focusing specifically on Hungarian art. Its mission is to showcase the rich cultural heritage and artistic achievements of Hungary.

Location

The museum is housed within the historic Buda Castle complex, a UNESCO World Heritage site. Its location provides a picturesque setting, overlooking the Danube River and offering stunning views of Budapest.

Collections

The Hungarian National Gallery houses a comprehensive collection of Hungarian art, spanning various periods and styles. The collection includes paintings, sculptures, prints, drawings, and decorative art objects. It features works by renowned Hungarian artists such as Mihály Munkácsy, József Rippl-Rónai, István Csók, and many others.

Highlights

The museum's permanent exhibitions are organized chronologically, allowing visitors to experience the development of Hungarian art over time. Highlights of the collection include medieval and

Renaissance artworks, Baroque paintings, 19th-century Hungarian realism, and modern and contemporary Hungarian art. The gallery also has a significant collection of works by Hungarian artists from the 20th century, including the avant-garde movements of the early 1900s.

Temporary Exhibitions

The Hungarian National Gallery hosts temporary exhibitions that explore specific themes, artists, or art movements. These exhibitions offer a fresh perspective and the opportunity to see artworks that are not part of the permanent collection.

Building and Architecture

The Hungarian National Gallery is located within the former Royal Palace, a magnificent architectural complex. The museum occupies several buildings within the palace complex, each with its own distinct architectural style, ranging from Gothic to Baroque and Neo-Classical.

Cultural Events and Activities

The museum regularly organizes cultural events, including lectures, workshops, concerts, and film screenings. These activities provide further insights into Hungarian art, history, and culture.

Museum of Applied Arts

The Museum of Applied Arts, known as Iparművészeti Múzeum in Hungarian, is a prominent museum in Budapest, Hungary, dedicated to the decorative arts, design, and applied arts. Here's more information about the Museum of Applied Arts:

History

The Museum of Applied Arts was established in 1872 and is one of the oldest museums of its kind in Europe. Its mission is to collect, preserve, and showcase decorative arts and design objects, both from Hungary and around the world.

Building and Architecture

The museum's building itself is a masterpiece of Hungarian architecture. Designed by Ödön Lechner and Gyula Pártos, it is a prime example of the Hungarian Art Nouveau style, often referred to as "Lechner-style" or "Hungarian Secession." The exterior of the building is adorned with colorful Zsolnay ceramic tiles, intricate brickwork, and unique architectural details.

Collections

The Museum of Applied Arts houses a vast collection of decorative arts, design objects, and applied arts. The collection spans a wide range of mediums, including ceramics, glassware, textiles, furniture, metalwork, jewelry, and more. The museum's holdings encompass works from various periods and styles, representing both Hungarian and international artists and craftsmen.

Hungarian Art Nouveau

The museum's collection includes an exceptional array of Hungarian Art Nouveau (Secession) pieces. These objects showcase the distinct style and craftsmanship of Hungarian artists during the late 19th and early 20th centuries. Visitors can admire beautiful ceramics, glassware, furniture, and decorative objects that exemplify the Art Nouveau aesthetic.

Special Exhibitions

In addition to its permanent collection, the Museum of Applied Arts hosts temporary exhibitions that focus on specific themes, artists, or design movements. These exhibitions provide a platform for exploring contemporary design trends, innovative approaches, and historical contexts within the field of applied arts.

Library and Research

The museum has a specialized library that houses a comprehensive collection of books, periodicals, and archival materials related to applied arts and design. It serves as a resource for researchers, scholars, and students interested in these fields.

Educational Programs and Events

The Museum of Applied Arts offers educational programs, workshops, and guided tours that cater to various age groups and interests. These activities aim to engage visitors and deepen their understanding of decorative arts, design history, and the creative process.

Holocaust Memorial Center

The Holocaust Memorial Center, known as Holokauszt Emlékközpont in Hungarian, is a significant museum and memorial in Budapest, Hungary, dedicated to commemorating the victims of the Holocaust, educating visitors about this dark chapter in history, and promoting tolerance and understanding. Here's more information about the Holocaust Memorial Center:

History and Location

The Holocaust Memorial Center was established in 2004 as a national institution to honor the memory of the Holocaust victims in Hungary. It is located in the former Páva Street Synagogue, which played a crucial role in the Jewish community before and during World War II.

Exhibitions

The center features permanent and temporary exhibitions that offer a comprehensive understanding of the Holocaust and its impact on

Hungarian Jews. The permanent exhibition takes visitors through the history of Hungarian Jewry, the rise of Nazism, the deportation and mass murder of Hungarian Jews, and the stories of survivors. Personal testimonies, photographs, artifacts, and multimedia presentations provide a poignant and immersive experience.

Páva Street Synagogue

The Holocaust Memorial Center is housed in the restored Páva Street Synagogue, which was once an important religious and cultural center for the Jewish community in Budapest. The building itself has historical significance and serves as a reminder of the vibrant Jewish life that existed before the Holocaust.

Memorial Wall and Garden

Adjacent to the museum is a tranquil garden with a Memorial Wall that bears the names of Hungarian Holocaust victims. The serene atmosphere provides visitors with a space for reflection and remembrance.

Educational Programs

The Holocaust Memorial Center offers educational programs, workshops, guided tours, and lectures aimed at promoting awareness, understanding, and tolerance. These activities engage visitors, particularly students, in learning about the Holocaust and its implications for society.

Research and Documentation

The center houses a research institute that focuses on Holocaust-related studies, documentation, and archival research. Scholars and researchers have access to valuable resources and materials for further study.

Events and Commemorations

The Holocaust Memorial Center hosts events, commemorative ceremonies, and lectures throughout the year to honor the victims and engage the community in discussions about the Holocaust, human rights, and tolerance.

House of Terror

The House of Terror, known as Terror Háza in Hungarian, is a museum located in Budapest, Hungary. It is a unique institution that focuses on the dark history of Hungary during the Nazi and Communist regimes. The museum is housed in the former headquarters of the secret police organizations of both periods, offering visitors an immersive and educational experience. Here's more information about the House of Terror:

History and Purpose

The House of Terror was established in 2002 with the aim of commemorating the victims and raising awareness of the atrocities committed by the Nazi and Communist regimes in Hungary. The museum seeks to provide insight into the experiences of those who suffered during these oppressive periods and to promote dialogue about the importance of democracy, freedom, and human rights.

Location and Building

The museum is situated at 60 Andrássy Avenue, a significant street in Budapest. The building itself played a significant role during the Nazi and Communist eras as the headquarters of the Hungarian Arrow Cross Party and the State Security Authority (ÁVH). Its imposing façade and historical significance contribute to the immersive experience within the museum.

Exhibitions

The House of Terror features thought-provoking exhibitions that depict the terror and totalitarianism of the Nazi and Communist regimes. The exhibits include photographs, personal stories, documents, audiovisual presentations, and authentic artifacts from the era. They provide a comprehensive understanding of the political oppression, surveillance, torture, and persecution that occurred during these periods.

The Basement

One of the most striking sections of the museum is its basement, which has been preserved to resemble the prison cells used by the ÁVH secret police. Visitors can explore the cramped cells, experience the chilling environment, and gain a visceral understanding of the conditions endured by political prisoners.

Memorial Wall and Garden

The museum's exterior features a memorial wall with the names of those who lost their lives or were affected by the Nazi and Communist regimes. Adjacent to the museum is a serene garden with statues and memorials dedicated to the victims, providing a place for reflection and remembrance.

Education and Events

The House of Terror offers educational programs, lectures, and events aimed at fostering a deeper understanding of Hungary's history and promoting dialogue about democracy, human rights, and totalitarianism.

Hospital in the Rock Nuclear Bunker Museum

The Hospital in the Rock Nuclear Bunker Museum, located in Budapest, Hungary, is a unique museum that offers a glimpse into Hungary's history during World War II and the Cold War era. It is situated in a natural cave system under Buda Castle and was originally built as a secret emergency hospital and shelter. Here's more information about the Hospital in the Rock Nuclear Bunker Museum:

History and Purpose

The Hospital in the Rock was originally established during World War II as a makeshift hospital in response to the bombings of Budapest. It was later expanded and reinforced during the Cold War period to serve as a nuclear bunker and emergency hospital in the event of a nuclear attack. The facility was top-secret and designed to provide medical care for wounded soldiers and civilians.

Bunker Infrastructure

The museum showcases the well-preserved underground complex, which includes a labyrinth of tunnels, rooms, and chambers that served various purposes during different periods. Visitors can explore the former hospital wards, operating rooms, a chapel, decontamination rooms, and even the living quarters for medical staff.

Exhibitions

The museum's exhibitions provide a historical context and insight into the conditions and challenges faced during times of war and potential nuclear threat. Through displays of medical equipment, photographs, documents, and multimedia presentations, visitors can learn about the medical procedures, living conditions, and the experiences of both medical staff and patients during wartime.

Cold War Era

The museum also focuses on the Cold War period and the arms race between the United States and the Soviet Union. It highlights the preparations made by Hungary to protect its citizens in the event of a nuclear attack and provides a glimpse into the tense political climate of the time.

Audio Guide

Visitors to the Hospital in the Rock can enhance their experience with an audio guide available in multiple languages. The audio guide provides detailed explanations, stories, and firsthand accounts, adding depth and context to the exhibits.

Guided Tours

The museum offers guided tours led by knowledgeable guides who provide additional insights and historical context. The guides share stories about the facility's history, the people who worked there, and the patients it served.

Education and Events

The Hospital in the Rock Nuclear Bunker Museum offers educational programs and events to engage visitors of all ages. These activities include workshops, lectures, and interactive presentations that delve deeper into the history and significance of the facility.

BUDAPEST TUNNELS

Budapest, Hungary, is a city with a rich history that includes a network of tunnels and underground passages that add to its intrigue and charm. These tunnels have various purposes, ranging from historical military fortifications to modern transportation systems. Here are some notable Budapest tunnels:

Buda Castle Labyrinth

The Buda Castle Labyrinth, also known as the Labyrinth of Buda Castle, is an intriguing underground complex located beneath Buda Castle Hill in Budapest, Hungary. This network of caves, tunnels, and cellars has a long and fascinating history that dates back centuries. Here are some key details about the Buda Castle Labyrinth:

Historical Origins

The caves and tunnels beneath Buda Castle Hill were formed over millions of years by the natural erosion of the limestone rock. These underground spaces were initially used as natural caves and later adapted by humans for various purposes.

Wine Cellars

During the Middle Ages, the caves served as wine cellars, providing an ideal environment for storing and aging wine. Hungarian wines, renowned for their quality, were stored in these cellars.

Military Use

Over the centuries, the caves and tunnels were used for military purposes. During the Middle Ages and the Ottoman era, they served as fortifications and secret escape routes for the castle's defenders.

World War II

During World War II, the Buda Castle Labyrinth was converted into an air raid shelter and military facility. It provided shelter for civilians during bombing raids and served as a hospital for the wounded.

Post-War Era

After World War II, the labyrinth fell into disrepair and was closed to the public. In the 1950s, it was used as a storage facility for wines and other goods.

Tourist Attraction

In the 1980s, the Buda Castle Labyrinth was reopened as a tourist attraction. It was renovated and transformed into an underground labyrinth filled with dark corridors, eerie chambers, and mysterious exhibits.

Themes and Exhibits

The labyrinth's underground passages now feature various exhibits and displays related to Hungarian folklore, history, and mythology. Visitors can explore the labyrinth, encountering displays of ancient Hungarian legends, mythical creatures, and historical figures.

Special Events

The Buda Castle Labyrinth also hosts special events, such as concerts, theatrical performances, and themed exhibitions, making it an immersive and interactive experience for visitors of all ages.

Historical and Cultural Significance

The Buda Castle Labyrinth provides a unique opportunity to delve into Budapest's past, uncovering the layers of history and folklore that have shaped the city's identity.

Szemlőhegyi Cave

The Szemlőhegyi Cave, also known as Szemlőhegy Cave (Szemlőhegyi barlang), is a magnificent natural cave system located in Budapest, Hungary. It is one of the most popular and accessible caves in the city, offering visitors a chance to explore stunning underground formations and geological wonders. Here are some key details about the Szemlőhegyi Cave:

Formation and Geological Features

The Szemlőhegyi Cave was formed millions of years ago through the erosion of limestone rocks. The cave is renowned for its impressive stalactites, stalagmites, flowstones, and various other unique formations created by the slow deposition of mineral-rich water.

Length and Exploration

The total length of the cave system is around 2,200 meters, with different sections offering different levels of difficulty for exploration. Guided tours are available, and visitors can explore a part of the cave that is open to the public.

Accessibility

Unlike some other caves that might require special equipment or expertise, the Szemlőhegyi Cave is relatively accessible to a wide range of visitors, making it a popular destination for families and tourists alike.

Guided Tours

To preserve the cave's delicate environment and ensure visitor safety, the cave is only accessible through guided tours. The tours are led by experienced guides who provide valuable information about the cave's geology, history, and ecology.

Underground Concerts

One of the unique features of the Szemlőhegyi Cave is that it serves as a venue for underground concerts and cultural events. The natural acoustics of the cave create a unique and enchanting atmosphere for performances.

Educational Center

The cave's visitor center offers educational exhibits and displays about cave formations, cave-dwelling animals, and the importance of cave conservation.

Temperature and Climate

The temperature inside the Szemlőhegyi Cave remains relatively constant throughout the year, making it a pleasant destination to visit in any season.

Conservation Efforts

To preserve the cave's natural beauty and protect its fragile ecosystem, strict regulations are in place to ensure responsible cave exploration and conservation.

Tunnel under Castle Hill

The Tunnel under Castle Hill, also known as the Castle Hill Cave, is an underground passage located beneath Buda Castle Hill in Budapest, Hungary. This tunnel has historical significance and served various purposes throughout its existence. Here are some key details about the Tunnel under Castle Hill:

Historical Origins

The Tunnel under Castle Hill has a history dating back to the Middle Ages. It was initially constructed as part of the castle's fortifications, providing a means of defense and escape during times of siege.

Military Use

During the Ottoman era, the tunnel served as a crucial escape route for the defenders of Buda Castle. In times of danger, soldiers and residents could use the tunnel to retreat safely to other parts of the city.

Air Raid Shelter

During World War II, the tunnel was converted into an air raid shelter and used to provide protection for civilians during bombing raids.

Connection to the Citadella

The tunnel connects Buda Castle Hill to the Citadella, a fortress situated atop Gellért Hill on the opposite side of the Danube River. This underground passage allowed for strategic movements and communication between the two fortifications.

Preservation and Accessibility

While the Tunnel under Castle Hill has historical significance, only a part of it is accessible to the public today. It is not fully open for regular tours, but visitors can explore certain sections that are open for guided visits.

Importance to Hungarian History

The tunnel is a physical reminder of the many historic events that took place in Budapest, reflecting its role as a city with a complex and rich past.

Heritage and Conservation

The tunnel is part of Budapest's cultural heritage, and efforts are made to preserve and protect its historical value.

Millennium Underground

The Millennium Underground, also known as Metro Line 1, is the oldest underground railway system in continental Europe and a significant part of Budapest's public transportation network. It holds historical and cultural significance as a remarkable engineering achievement and a symbol of Hungary's commitment to progress during the late 19th century. Here are some key details about the Millennium Underground:

Inauguration

The Millennium Underground was inaugurated on May 2, 1896, to commemorate the 1,000th anniversary of the Hungarian conquest of the Carpathian Basin, which took place in 896 AD.

Design and Architecture

The line was designed by engineers Gyula Rochlitz, Henrik Báthory, and Vilmos Zsigmondy. Its architectural style reflects the ornate Art Nouveau and eclectic architectural influences of the period.

Route

The Millennium Underground runs between Vörösmarty Square in the city center of Pest and Heroes' Square (Hősök tere) in City Park. It covers a distance of about 4.4 kilometers (2.7 miles) and consists of 11 stations.

Original Rolling Stock

The original rolling stock of the Millennium Underground featured wooden carriages with open windows. Over the years, the rolling stock has been modernized, but the original stations and architectural elements have been preserved.

UNESCO World Heritage

In recognition of its historical and cultural significance, the Millennium Underground, along with Andrássy Avenue (the boulevard along which it runs), was designated a UNESCO World Heritage Site in 2002.

Role in Urban Development

The construction of the Millennium Underground played a crucial role in the urban development of Budapest. It facilitated easier and faster transportation for residents and contributed to the growth of the city.

Art Nouveau Stations

The stations of the Millennium Underground are known for their distinctive Art Nouveau architectural style, characterized by decorative motifs, colorful tiles, and wrought iron details.

Historic Landmarks

The line passes by several historic landmarks, including the Hungarian State Opera House, the House of Terror Museum, and Heroes' Square, where it terminates.

Batthyány Square Metro Station

Batthyány Square Metro Station is a significant transportation hub and one of the key metro stations in Budapest, Hungary. It is located in the Buda side of the city and serves as an essential link between different parts of Budapest. Here are some key details about Batthyány Square Metro Station:

Location

Batthyány Square Metro Station is situated in the heart of Buda, near the Danube River, and is named after Batthyány Square, the central square in the area.

Metro Line

The station is part of Metro Line 2, also known as the Red Line, which runs between Déli pályaudvar (Southern Railway Station) and Örs vezér tere.

Accessibility

Batthyány Square Metro Station is easily accessible and well-connected to other modes of transportation, including buses and trams.

Design and Architecture

The station's design reflects the unique architectural style of Budapest's metro system, which features bright, colorful tiles, decorative motifs, and Art Nouveau elements.

Batthyány Square

The square itself is a bustling area with various shops, restaurants, and amenities, making the metro station a vibrant and lively place for commuters and visitors.

Nearby Attractions

Batthyány Square is close to several notable attractions, including the historic Batthyány Square Church and the Hungarian Parliament Building, both of which are within walking distance from the metro station.

Convenient Location

Due to its central location and accessibility, Batthyány Square Metro Station is a popular starting point for tourists exploring Buda's historic landmarks and attractions.

Connections

The station is well-connected to other parts of the city, making it easy for commuters and travelers to reach popular destinations in Budapest.

Déli Railway Station Tunnel

The Déli Railway Station Tunnel, also known as Déli pályaudvar, is an underground pedestrian passage located at Déli Railway Station in Budapest, Hungary. As one of the major railway stations in the city, Déli Railway Station serves as a vital transportation hub connecting Budapest with other parts of Hungary and neighboring countries. Here are some key details about the Déli Railway Station Tunnel:

Location

The Déli Railway Station Tunnel is situated beneath Déli pályaudvar, one of Budapest's three main railway stations. It is located on the Buda side of the city, providing railway connections to destinations in Western Hungary, Croatia, and beyond.

Pedestrian Tunnel

The tunnel primarily serves as a pedestrian passage connecting the various platforms and railway tracks of Déli Railway Station. It offers a convenient and safe way for passengers to move between different platforms and access their trains.

Déli Railway Station

Déli pályaudvar is an essential transportation hub in Budapest, serving as a gateway for travelers arriving in or departing from the Buda side of the city. It offers connections to cities like Vienna, Bratislava, Zagreb, and more.

Accessibility

The tunnel is accessible to all passengers, including those with mobility challenges. It provides a seamless and efficient transfer between trains and platforms.

Architectural Features

While primarily functional in design, the tunnel may also feature practical amenities such as ticket counters, information boards, and seating areas for passengers.

Connection to the City

Déli Railway Station is well-connected to Budapest's public transportation network, including the metro, buses, and trams. This makes it easy for passengers to reach other parts of the city from the railway station.

Historic Building

Déli Railway Station itself is an impressive historic building with distinctive architectural features, serving as a cultural and transportation landmark in Budapest.

BUDAPEST CHURCHES

Budapest is home to several beautiful and historically significant churches that reflect the city's rich religious and architectural heritage. These churches showcase various architectural styles, ranging from Romanesque and Gothic to Baroque and Neoclassical. Here are some of the notable churches you should consider visiting during your time in Budapest:

St. Stephen's Basilica (Szent István Bazilika)

St. Stephen's Basilica, or Szent István Bazilika in Hungarian, is one of the most prominent and impressive religious landmarks in Budapest. Named after Hungary's first king, St. Stephen, the basilica holds great historical and spiritual significance for the country. Here's a closer look at this stunning neoclassical masterpiece:

Architecture

St. Stephen's Basilica was designed by architect József Hild in the mid-19th century, but it was completed by Miklós Ybl after Hild's death. The basilica is an excellent example of neoclassical architecture, with its grand proportions, elegant façade, and a monumental dome that rises 96 meters (315 feet) into the Budapest skyline.

Interior

The interior of St. Stephen's Basilica is equally impressive. The nave is adorned with beautiful stucco work, paintings, and intricate details. The main altar features a magnificent marble baldachin, and the sanctuary houses the relics of St. Stephen, including his mummified right hand, which is kept in a glass case for visitors to see.

Holy Right Hand of St. Stephen

The basilica's most treasured relic is the Holy Right Hand of St. Stephen, Hungary's patron saint. The mummified hand, which is believed to have miraculous powers, is displayed in a chapel inside the basilica. It attracts pilgrims and visitors from around the world who come to pay their respects.

Organ and Music

St. Stephen's Basilica is known for its exceptional acoustics, making it a popular venue for concerts and musical performances. The basilica's organ is one of the largest in Hungary and a centerpiece during musical events.

Panoramic Views

For a stunning panoramic view of Budapest, visitors can climb the 364 stairs (or take the elevator) to the dome's observation deck. The breathtaking views of the city and the Danube River from this vantage point are well worth the effort.

Religious Services and Events

St. Stephen's Basilica continues to be an active place of worship, hosting regular religious services, including Mass and other ceremonies. Additionally, the basilica hosts various cultural events, such as organ concerts and choir performances, attracting both locals and tourists.

Accessibility

The basilica is centrally located on Szent István tér (St. Stephen's Square) in Pest, making it easily accessible from various parts of the city. It is a popular stop for both guided tours and independent travelers exploring Budapest.

Matthias Church (Mátyás-templom)

Matthias Church, also known as Mátyás-templom in Hungarian, is one of the most beautiful and historically significant churches in Budapest. Located in the Buda Castle District, the church is a symbol of Hungary's rich history and architectural heritage. Here's what you need to know about Matthias Church:

Architecture

Matthias Church is a masterpiece of Gothic architecture, with some elements of Romanesque and Baroque styles as well. The church has undergone several renovations and expansions over the centuries, which have contributed to its unique and eclectic design.

Historical Significance

The church's history dates back to the 13th century when a Romanesque church was built on the site. During the reign of King Matthias in the 15th century, the church was rebuilt in a grand Gothic style and became a coronation church for Hungarian kings. Numerous royal weddings and coronations took place within its walls.

Colorful Tiled Roof

One of the most striking features of Matthias Church is its colorful, ornate tiled roof. The roof tiles are arranged in a distinctive pattern, creating an eye-catching mosaic of colors. The motifs on the roof include the double-cross of Lorraine, representing the Hungarian coat of arms.

Interior

The interior of Matthias Church is just as impressive as its exterior. The church's nave features a beautiful vaulted ceiling and intricate stained glass windows that depict various religious scenes. The interior is adorned with rich decorations, including frescoes, sculptures, and religious artifacts.

Organ and Music

Matthias Church houses a magnificent organ, renowned for its powerful and melodious tones. The church hosts organ concerts and musical performances that enchant visitors with the harmonious sounds of this historic instrument.

Religious Services and Events

Matthias Church remains an active place of worship, holding regular religious services and ceremonies. Additionally, the church hosts special events, including concerts, art exhibitions, and cultural festivals, which attract both locals and tourists.

Fisherman's Bastion

Adjacent to Matthias Church is the famous Fisherman's Bastion, a neo-Gothic terrace with seven ornate towers offering panoramic views of the Danube River, the Parliament building, and Pest. The bastion was constructed in the late 19th century and complements the beauty of Matthias Church.

Great Synagogue (Dohány Street Synagogue)

The Great Synagogue, also known as the Dohány Street Synagogue (Dohány utcai zsinagóga) in Hungarian, is one of the most prominent and historically significant synagogues in Budapest and Europe. It is a symbol of Hungary's rich Jewish heritage and serves as a center for Jewish religious and cultural activities. Here's what you should know about the Great Synagogue:

Architecture

The Great Synagogue was designed by the Viennese architect Ludwig Förster in the mid-19th century. It is an excellent example of Moorish Revival architecture, with a mix of Romantic and Islamic architectural elements. The facade features beautiful arches, decorative motifs, and two onion-shaped domes.

Size and Capacity

The Great Synagogue is one of the largest synagogues in the world, with a capacity of up to 3,000 people. Its vast interior can accommodate a large congregation and is adorned with intricate decorations and religious symbols.

Holocaust Memorial

The courtyard of the Great Synagogue houses a moving Holocaust Memorial, known as the Emanuel Tree. This metal weeping willow sculpture is dedicated to the memory of Hungarian Jews who lost their lives during the Holocaust. The leaves of the tree are inscribed with the names of Holocaust victims.

Jewish Museum

Adjacent to the Great Synagogue is the Jewish Museum, which houses a collection of Jewish artifacts, religious objects, historical documents, and artwork. The museum provides insight into the history and culture of Hungarian Jewry.

Heroes' Temple

Within the complex, there is a separate Heroes' Temple, also known as the Raoul Wallenberg Memorial Park. It honors the memory of Raoul Wallenberg, a Swedish diplomat who saved thousands of Hungarian Jews during the Holocaust.

Religious Services

The Great Synagogue remains an active place of worship, hosting regular religious services, holiday celebrations, and life-cycle events, such as weddings and bar mitzvahs.

Concerts and Events

The Great Synagogue is also a venue for concerts, cultural events, and educational programs, attracting visitors interested in Jewish music, dance, and traditions.

Open to Visitors

The Great Synagogue welcomes visitors of all backgrounds to explore its historic and cultural significance. Guided tours are available, providing insights into the synagogue's architecture, history, and Jewish traditions.

St. Anne's Church (Szent Anna-templom)

St. Anne's Church, known as Szent Anna-templom in Hungarian, is a charming and historically significant church located in the Buda Castle District of Budapest. While it may not be as well-known as some of the city's other prominent churches, it holds a unique beauty and historical value. Here's what you should know about St. Anne's Church:

Architecture

St. Anne's Church is a fine example of Gothic architecture, dating back to the 14th century. It features typical Gothic elements, including pointed arches, ribbed vaults, and slender columns. The church has a simple and unpretentious exterior that blends harmoniously with its surroundings.

History and Renovations

The church has a rich history, with several renovations and additions over the centuries. It was originally constructed in the 14th century, but its current appearance is the result of later restorations. Despite its age, St. Anne's Church has retained its authentic Gothic character.

Location and Setting

St. Anne's Church is nestled among the historic buildings of the Buda Castle District, creating a picturesque and tranquil ambiance. Its location near Matthias Church and the Fisherman's Bastion makes it a convenient stop for visitors exploring this charming part of Budapest.

Unique Interior

While the church's exterior may appear relatively modest, its interior holds some surprises. St. Anne's Church boasts beautiful stained glass windows and unique frescoes that add color and warmth to the space. The charming simplicity of the interior contributes to the church's serene atmosphere.

Nearby Attractions

St. Anne's Church is located near several other attractions in the Buda Castle District. Visitors can easily combine a visit to the church with exploring Matthias Church, the Fisherman's Bastion, and the historic streets and squares of the area.

Accessibility

Due to its location within the Buda Castle District, access to St. Anne's Church may involve some walking and navigating through narrow streets. However, the effort is well worth it for those seeking a quieter and less crowded spot for reflection and admiration.

St. Michael's Church (Szent Mihály-templom)

St. Michael's Church, or Szent Mihály-templom in Hungarian, is a beautiful Baroque-style church located in the Buda Castle District of Budapest. Although not as well-known as some of the city's other iconic churches, it holds historical and architectural significance and is worth a visit for those exploring the historic heart of Budapest. Here's what you should know about St. Michael's Church:

Architecture

St. Michael's Church was constructed in the late 17th century in the Baroque architectural style. It features a classical Baroque facade with intricate stucco decorations and a soaring bell tower. The church's design reflects the grandeur and elegance characteristic of the Baroque period.

Location and Setting

The church is situated near the heart of the Buda Castle District, making it easily accessible for visitors exploring this historic area. Its location amidst the castle's medieval and Baroque buildings adds to the charm of the surroundings.

Historical Significance

St. Michael's Church has witnessed various historical events over the centuries. It played a role in the life of the Hungarian royal court during the Habsburg period, and its congregation has been an integral part of Budapest's religious and cultural landscape.

Interior Decorations

The interior of St. Michael's Church is adorned with stunning Baroque decorations, including ornate altars, statues, and frescoes. The church's interior exudes an atmosphere of elegance and devotion, inviting visitors to admire its beauty and historical significance.

Religious Services and Events

While St. Michael's Church is a popular destination for visitors, it remains an active place of worship. The church hosts regular religious services, including Mass and other ceremonies, providing a place for the local community to gather and celebrate their faith.

Accessibility

Like many of the attractions in the Buda Castle District, access to St. Michael's Church may involve some walking on cobbled streets and steps. However, the journey through this historic area adds to the overall experience of visiting the church.

Church of Our Lady (Boldogasszony-templom) in Óbuda

The Church of Our Lady, also known as Boldogasszony-templom in Hungarian, is a significant historical and religious site located in Óbuda, a district of Budapest. The church is one of the oldest in the city and holds a special place in Hungary's religious heritage. Here's what you should know about the Church of Our Lady in Óbuda:

Historical Significance

The Church of Our Lady has a long and storied history, dating back to the 11th century. It is one of the oldest churches in Budapest and has witnessed various historical events over the centuries.

Romanesque Architecture

The original church was built in the Romanesque architectural style, which was prevalent during the medieval period. While the church has undergone several renovations and reconstructions over the centuries, some elements of its Romanesque past can still be seen in its design.

Location in Óbuda

The church is situated in the Óbuda district of Budapest, an area known for its historical significance and charming atmosphere. Óbuda has preserved much of its medieval and Baroque architecture, providing a unique backdrop for the church.

Renovations and Restorations

Throughout its history, the Church of Our Lady has undergone numerous renovations and restorations to preserve its architectural and historical value. These efforts have helped maintain the church's original character while adapting it to changing times.

Religious Services and Events

The Church of Our Lady continues to be an active place of worship, hosting regular religious services, including Mass and other ceremonies. It also holds special events and celebrations, particularly during religious holidays and local festivals.

Nearby Attractions

Visitors to the Church of Our Lady can also explore other attractions in Óbuda, such as the historical streets, squares, and museums that provide insight into the district's rich history and cultural heritage.

St. Elizabeth of Hungary Church (Erzsébet-templom)

St. Elizabeth of Hungary Church, or Erzsébet-templom in Hungarian, is a delightful church located in the heart of Budapest. It is dedicated to St. Elizabeth of Hungary, also known as St. Elizabeth of Thuringia, who was a princess and a symbol of compassion and charity. Here's what you should know about St. Elizabeth of Hungary Church:

Architecture

St. Elizabeth of Hungary Church is an eclectic building that showcases a blend of architectural styles. It was constructed in the late 19th century and features a combination of Romantic and Neo-Gothic elements, creating a unique and charming facade.

Location

The church is situated near the vibrant city center of Budapest, making it easily accessible for both locals and tourists. Its central location makes it a convenient stop while exploring other attractions and landmarks in the city.

Dedication to St. Elizabeth

The church is named after St. Elizabeth of Hungary, who was a devout Catholic known for her acts of charity and kindness toward the poor and sick. Her life and dedication to helping others have made her a beloved figure in the Christian tradition.

Interior

The interior of St. Elizabeth of Hungary Church is characterized by its simplicity and elegance. The church's nave is adorned with beautiful stained glass windows and religious artwork, creating a tranquil and meditative atmosphere for worshippers and visitors alike.

Religious Services

St. Elizabeth of Hungary Church remains an active place of worship, hosting regular religious services, including Mass and other ceremonies. The church welcomes both locals and visitors to participate in its religious activities.

Social Outreach

In keeping with the spirit of St. Elizabeth's charitable work, the church is involved in various social outreach programs and initiatives aimed at helping those in need in the local community.

Nearby Attractions

The church's central location allows visitors to easily explore other nearby attractions, such as the Hungarian State Opera House, Andrassy Avenue, and numerous shops, cafes, and restaurants.

ECLECTIC NEIGHBORHOODS

Budapest is a city known for its diverse and eclectic neighborhoods, each with its own unique character and atmosphere. Exploring these neighborhoods allows you to experience different aspects of the city's culture, history, and local life. Here are a few eclectic neighborhoods in Budapest worth exploring:

District VII (Erzsébetváros)

Located in the heart of Budapest, District VII, also known as the Jewish Quarter, is a vibrant and eclectic neighborhood. It is known for its lively atmosphere, street art, quirky ruin bars, alternative cafes, and a thriving nightlife scene. The area also boasts historical sites like the Great Synagogue and the Jewish Museum, offering a blend of history and contemporary culture.

District VIII (Józsefváros)

Józsefváros is a diverse neighborhood with a mix of residential areas, cultural landmarks, and universities. It is home to the stunning New York Palace, the National Museum, and the Hungarian Natural History Museum. The neighborhood offers a lively atmosphere, with trendy cafes, cozy restaurants, and local markets.

District IX (Ferencváros)

Situated on the Pest side of the city, Ferencváros is a dynamic neighborhood with a mix of modern developments and historical charm. It is home to the Budapest University of Technology and Economics and the Palace of Arts (Müpa Budapest). The area has a growing food scene, including trendy restaurants and local markets.

District XIII (Újlipótváros)

Újlipótváros is a residential neighborhood located on the Pest side, along the Danube River. It is known for its tree-lined streets, art nouveau architecture, and a lively atmosphere. The neighborhood offers a mix of trendy cafes, boutique shops, and local markets, such as Lehel Market.

District VI (Terézváros)

Terézváros is a central district that combines elegant architecture with a bohemian vibe. It is home to the iconic Andrássy Avenue, lined with upscale shops, cafes, and the Hungarian State Opera House. The neighborhood also offers a range of restaurants, cultural venues, and unique boutiques.

District V (Belváros-Lipótváros)

Belváros-Lipótváros, also known as the Inner City, is the historic center of Budapest. It features grand buildings, historic landmarks, and pedestrian-friendly streets. The neighborhood offers a mix of upscale shops, elegant cafes, and fine dining options. It is home to attractions like the Hungarian Parliament, St. Stephen's Basilica, and Váci Street, a popular shopping destination.

STREET ART AND GRAFFITI

Budapest has a thriving street art and graffiti scene that adds a vibrant and artistic touch to the city's urban landscape. The presence of street art can be found in various neighborhoods throughout Budapest, turning some of its walls, buildings, and public spaces into open-air galleries. Here's what you can expect to find regarding street art and graffiti in Budapest:

District VII (Jewish Quarter)

District VII, also known as the Jewish Quarter, is one of Budapest's most vibrant and eclectic neighborhoods. Located in the Pest side of the city, this area has a fascinating history and a unique atmosphere that draws both locals and tourists alike. Here's what you can expect to find in District VII:

Jewish Heritage

The Jewish Quarter has a significant Jewish heritage, and it's home to several historical landmarks. The Dohány Street Synagogue, also known as the Great Synagogue, is the largest synagogue in Europe and a must-visit attraction. Nearby, you'll find the Jewish Museum, the Holocaust Memorial Center, and the Tree of Life Memorial.

Ruin Bars and Nightlife

The district is renowned for its ruin bars, which are unique drinking spots located in old, abandoned buildings or courtyards. Szimpla Kert, one of the first ruin bars in the city, is an iconic spot where you can enjoy a drink amidst quirky and artistic interiors. The ruin bars often host live music, film screenings, and other events, making them a favorite destination for Budapest's nightlife.

Street Art and Graffiti

District VII is a hub for street art and graffiti. Its walls are adorned with colorful murals, abstract paintings, and thought-provoking artworks. Kazinczy Street and Gozsdu Courtyard, in particular, are known for their artistic flair and vibrant atmosphere.

Eclectic Food Scene

The Jewish Quarter offers an array of dining options, catering to various tastes and preferences. You can find traditional Hungarian eateries, trendy cafes, international cuisine, and vegetarian/vegan restaurants. Don't miss the chance to try local street food and traditional Jewish dishes like falafel and chimney cake.

Unique Shops and Boutiques

The district is also known for its unique shops and boutiques, offering vintage clothing, antiques, handmade crafts, and contemporary designs. It's an excellent place to find one-of-a-kind souvenirs and gifts to take home.

Gozsdu Udvar

Gozsdu Udvar, a bustling passageway filled with restaurants, cafes, and shops, connects Király Street and Dob Street. It's a lively spot during the day and night, with a mix of locals and tourists enjoying the vibrant atmosphere.

Street Markets and Events

District VII hosts various street markets and cultural events, especially during weekends and holidays. These markets often feature local crafts, artisanal products, vintage items, and street food, offering a fantastic opportunity to immerse yourself in Budapest's local culture.

Kazinczy Street

Kazinczy Street is one of the central and most vibrant streets in Budapest's District VII, the Jewish Quarter. It is one of the main arteries of the neighborhood and a popular destination for both locals and tourists. Known for its lively atmosphere, Kazinczy Street offers a diverse range of activities, including bars, restaurants, street art, and cultural experiences. Here's what you can explore on Kazinczy Street:

Ruin Bars

Kazinczy Street is home to several famous ruin bars, making it a hotspot for Budapest's nightlife. These bars are unique in that they are set up in abandoned buildings, creating an eclectic and artsy ambiance. Szimpla Kert, one of the most well-known ruin bars in the city, is located on this street. It features multiple rooms, each with its own theme and decorations, making it a fascinating place to explore.

Street Art and Murals

Like much of District VII, Kazinczy Street is adorned with impressive street art and murals. The buildings' walls are often covered with colorful graffiti and artworks, showcasing the neighborhood's vibrant and artistic character.

Kazinczy Street Food Court

For food enthusiasts, the Kazinczy Street Food Court is a must-visit spot. This area is filled with a variety of food stalls and trucks offering a diverse range of culinary delights, including Hungarian street food, international cuisine, and vegetarian options.

Cultural Events

Kazinczy Street often hosts cultural events, live performances, and parties. Keep an eye out for flyers and posters advertising concerts, art exhibitions, and other activities taking place in the area.

Boutiques and Shops

The street is dotted with boutiques and shops selling everything from vintage clothing to unique handmade items. It's a great place to find souvenirs or gifts that reflect Budapest's artsy and creative vibe.

Street Markets

On certain days, Kazinczy Street hosts street markets where local vendors and artisans sell their products. These markets offer a great opportunity to discover local crafts, artwork, and other unique items.

Street Photography

With its lively atmosphere and colorful surroundings, Kazinczy Street is a paradise for street photographers. The street's architecture, street art, and the hustle and bustle of daily life create captivating photo opportunities.

Gozsdu Courtyard

Gozsdu Courtyard, also known as Gozsdu Udvar in Hungarian, is a vibrant and lively passageway located in the heart of Budapest's District VII, the Jewish Quarter. It is one of the most popular destinations in the neighborhood, offering a unique blend of cultural experiences, dining options, nightlife, and a lively atmosphere. Here's what you can expect to find in Gozsdu Courtyard:

Dining and Nightlife

Gozsdu Courtyard is a hub for restaurants, cafes, bars, and pubs, making it an excellent spot to enjoy a meal or a night out. The courtyard is filled with diverse dining options, ranging from traditional Hungarian cuisine to international dishes. It's a perfect place to indulge in the city's culinary delights or to unwind with a drink in a vibrant setting.

Outdoor Seating

Many of the establishments in Gozsdu Courtyard offer outdoor seating, allowing visitors to enjoy their meals or drinks while immersed in the bustling atmosphere of the passageway. During the warmer months, the outdoor areas are particularly popular, creating a lively and social environment.

Cultural Events

Gozsdu Courtyard hosts various cultural events and performances throughout the year. These events may include live music, art exhibitions, theater shows, and more. Check the event schedule to see if there's anything happening during your visit.

Shops and Boutiques

The courtyard is also home to a variety of shops and boutiques, selling everything from unique souvenirs to local crafts and artisanal products. It's a great place to find gifts or mementos that reflect the creative spirit of Budapest.

Gozsdu Weekend Market

On weekends, the courtyard often hosts a popular market, attracting locals and tourists alike. The market features stalls selling fresh produce, handmade crafts, vintage items, and delicious street food, creating a vibrant and colorful atmosphere.

Art and Murals

Like much of District VII, Gozsdu Courtyard features impressive street art and murals, adding to the area's artistic flair. The walls are often adorned with colorful graffiti and imaginative artworks, providing a feast for the eyes as you explore the passageway.

Social Gathering Spot

Gozsdu Courtyard is a social hub where both locals and tourists come together to enjoy the lively atmosphere. Whether it's daytime or nighttime, the courtyard buzzes with energy, making it a popular meeting point in the Jewish Quarter.

Ruin Bars Street Art

Ruin bars are a unique and iconic feature of Budapest's nightlife scene. These bars are set up in abandoned or derelict buildings, typically located in the city's District VII, also known as the Jewish Quarter. Ruin bars have become an essential part of Budapest's cultural identity, offering a one-of-a-kind experience that combines creativity, history, and a lively atmosphere. Here's what you should know about ruin bars:

Concept and History

The concept of ruin bars originated in the early 2000s when entrepreneurs and artists saw the potential in repurposing abandoned buildings and turning them into unconventional drinking spots. These buildings were often left empty after World War II or during Hungary's transition from socialism to a market economy. Instead of demolishing them, creative minds transformed these neglected spaces into vibrant and unique bars.

Eclectic Decor

Ruin bars are known for their eclectic and artsy decor. Inside, you'll find a mishmash of vintage furniture, quirky decorations, retro items, and various art installations. Each room may have a distinct theme, creating a maze-like atmosphere that invites exploration.

Abandoned Courtyards

Many ruin bars feature open-air courtyards, which offer a fantastic space to socialize, relax, and enjoy drinks under the stars. These courtyards often host live music performances, DJs, and other events, adding to the bars' lively ambiance.

Diverse Music

Ruin bars cater to a wide range of musical tastes. You can expect to hear anything from electronic beats and indie tunes to jazz, rock, and even live performances. The diversity of music adds to the vibrant and inclusive nature of these bars.

Affordable Drinks

Ruin bars are known for their reasonable prices, making them popular among locals and budget-conscious travelers alike. You can enjoy a variety of beverages, from local Hungarian wines and craft beers to creative cocktails, without breaking the bank.

Social and International Atmosphere

Ruin bars attract a diverse crowd of locals and tourists from around the world. This international atmosphere fosters a sense of community, making it easy to strike up conversations with fellow patrons.

Szimpla Kert

One of the most famous ruin bars in Budapest is Szimpla Kert, located on Kazinczy Street. It is often considered the pioneer of the ruin bar movement and continues to be a popular hotspot for both daytime and nighttime gatherings.

Urban Art Galleries

Urban art galleries are spaces that celebrate and showcase street art and other forms of urban contemporary art in a curated and controlled setting. Unlike traditional art galleries, which typically feature more traditional art forms, urban art galleries focus on the works of street artists, graffiti artists, and other urban creatives. These galleries play a crucial role in elevating street art to the status of fine art, providing a platform for artists to exhibit their works and connecting them with art enthusiasts and collectors. Here's what you can expect from urban art galleries:

Exhibition Spaces

Urban art galleries feature exhibition spaces where artists display their artworks. These spaces may include indoor gallery areas, outdoor walls for murals, and sometimes even entire warehouses or buildings transformed into exhibition venues.

Rotating Exhibits

Urban art galleries often have rotating exhibits, showcasing different artists and art styles at different times. This dynamic approach keeps the gallery fresh and exciting for repeat visitors.

Curated Shows

Curators in urban art galleries carefully select and curate the artworks to create cohesive and visually compelling exhibitions. This curation process ensures that the gallery's theme and message resonate with the audience.

Diverse Styles and Mediums

Urban art encompasses a wide range of styles and mediums, including graffiti, stencil art, street photography, installations, and more. Urban art galleries embrace this diversity, giving visitors the opportunity to explore different forms of contemporary urban expression.

Art Sales and Collecting

Urban art galleries often offer artworks for sale, catering to both art collectors and enthusiasts. Visitors can purchase original pieces, prints, or other merchandise featuring the artists' work.

Events and Workshops

Some urban art galleries organize events, workshops, and talks to engage the local community and provide insights into the urban art scene. Workshops may include street art classes or opportunities for visitors to create their own urban art.

Showcasing Emerging Artists

Urban art galleries often serve as a platform for emerging artists, providing them with exposure and opportunities to establish their presence in the art world.

Street Art Festivals

Street art festivals are vibrant and dynamic events that celebrate the creativity and artistic expression of local and international street artists. These festivals provide a platform for artists to showcase their talents, transforming public spaces into colorful and captivating open-air galleries. Street art festivals have gained popularity worldwide, and Budapest is no exception. The city hosts various street art festivals, attracting artists and visitors alike. Here's what you can expect from these festivals in Budapest:

Showcase of Local and International Talent

Street art festivals in Budapest bring together a diverse mix of artists, both local and international. This convergence of talent creates a rich tapestry of artistic styles, techniques, and cultural influences, enriching the city's urban landscape.

Large-Scale Murals and Art Installations

During the festivals, artists often work on large-scale murals and art installations in designated areas across the city. These impressive works of art can be found on the sides of buildings, walls, bridges, and even on urban infrastructure, turning the city into an open-air art gallery.

Artistic Collaborations

Street art festivals encourage collaboration between artists, fostering a sense of community within the artistic community. It's not uncommon to see artists working together on joint projects or exchanging ideas during these events.

Engaging the Public

Street art festivals aim to engage the public and create an interactive experience. Some festivals may include workshops, live art demonstrations, and opportunities for visitors to participate in street art projects.

Cultural Exchange

International street artists participating in these festivals bring their unique perspectives and artistic traditions, creating a cultural exchange that enriches the local art scene and fosters cross-cultural understanding.

Revitalizing Urban Spaces

Street art festivals contribute to the revitalization of neglected or underutilized urban spaces. By transforming these spaces into vibrant works of art, the festivals breathe new life into the city and encourage public appreciation of art.

Social and Community Events

Street art festivals often feature social events, parties, and gatherings that bring artists and art enthusiasts together. These events create a festive and inclusive atmosphere, making the festivals enjoyable for people of all ages and backgrounds.

BARS AND NIGHTLIFE

Ruin Bars

Ruin bars, also known as ruin pubs, are a unique and popular aspect of Budapest's nightlife scene. These establishments are characterized by their eclectic, bohemian atmosphere and their location in old, abandoned buildings or courtyards. Here's more information about ruin bars in Budapest:

Origins

Ruin bars emerged in the early 2000s as a response to the abundance of abandoned buildings in Budapest's historic Jewish Quarter. Entrepreneurs and artists saw an opportunity to transform these neglected spaces into vibrant and alternative venues, giving rise to the concept of ruin bars.

Atmospheric Decor

Ruin bars are known for their quirky and artistic interior design. The spaces often feature mismatched furniture, vintage decor, street art, and recycled materials. The creative atmosphere adds to the unique charm of these establishments.

Diverse Venues

Budapest has numerous ruin bars scattered throughout the city, but the majority are concentrated in the Jewish Quarter and District VII.

Each ruin bar has its own distinct style and ambiance, catering to different tastes and preferences.

Garden Areas

Many ruin bars have spacious courtyards or garden areas, providing an open-air setting for visitors to relax, socialize, and enjoy drinks. These outdoor spaces often feature additional seating, bars, and live performances during warmer months.

Live Music and Events

Ruin bars are known for their vibrant nightlife and entertainment offerings. Many venues host live music performances, DJ sets, open mic nights, art exhibitions, and cultural events. The eclectic programming ensures there's always something happening in these dynamic spaces.

Affordable Drinks

Ruin bars are generally known for their affordable drink prices compared to more upscale establishments. It's common to find a wide selection of local and international beers, craft cocktails, and Hungarian wines at reasonable prices.

Social Hubs

Ruin bars attract both locals and tourists, making them lively social hubs where people from various backgrounds come together. They offer a relaxed and inclusive environment, fostering a sense of community and camaraderie.

Pub Crawls

Pub crawls are a popular and fun way to experience the nightlife in many cities, including Budapest. A pub crawl typically involves a guided tour that takes participants to multiple bars and pubs, allowing them to sample a variety of drinks, socialize with other participants, and enjoy the vibrant atmosphere of the city's nightlife. Here's what you should know about pub crawls in Budapest:

Organized Tours

Pub crawls in Budapest are often organized by local tour companies or nightlife guides. These tours usually start at a designated meeting point, and participants are accompanied by an enthusiastic and knowledgeable guide who leads the group to the best bars and pubs in the city.

Group Experience

Pub crawls are social events, and they are a fantastic way to meet fellow travelers and locals who are looking to have a good time. The group dynamic creates a lively and enjoyable atmosphere, making pub crawls perfect for solo travelers or groups of friends looking to make new connections.

Visiting Trendy Spots

The pub crawl route typically includes some of the trendiest and most popular bars and pubs in Budapest. These venues often have unique themes, eclectic decor, and a wide range of drinks to choose from, ensuring a diverse and exciting experience for participants.

Free or Discounted Drinks

Many pub crawls offer perks like free shots or discounted drinks at the participating venues. This can be a great way to sample local specialties or try out unique cocktails without breaking the bank.

Safety and Convenience

Participating in a pub crawl with a guide adds an extra layer of safety, especially if you're not familiar with the city. The guide can also help with logistics, such as navigating the nightlife scene, ensuring everyone stays together, and providing useful tips for a memorable night out.

Themed Pub Crawls

In addition to general pub crawls, Budapest also offers themed pub crawls catering to specific interests, such as craft beer crawls, cocktail-focused crawls, or even Halloween or holiday-themed crawls.

Age Restrictions

Some pub crawls have age restrictions, so it's essential to check the details and make sure you meet the requirements before joining.

When participating in a pub crawl, it's important to drink responsibly and look out for your fellow participants. Remember to stay hydrated, pace yourself, and be mindful of local customs and laws regarding alcohol consumption.

Live Music Venues

Budapest boasts a lively live music scene, with various venues offering a diverse range of musical genres and performances. Whether you're into jazz, rock, classical, or electronic music, there are venues to suit every taste. Here are some popular live music venues in Budapest:

A38 Ship

One of Budapest's most iconic music venues, A38 Ship is a converted Ukrainian stone-carrier ship docked on the Danube River. It hosts concerts of various genres, including rock, electronic, jazz, and world music. The unique setting and acoustics make it a favorite among locals and tourists alike.

Budapest Jazz Club

As the name suggests, Budapest Jazz Club is dedicated to jazz music and features performances by both local and international jazz artists. The cozy and intimate atmosphere creates a perfect setting for jazz enthusiasts.

Akvárium Klub

Akvárium Klub is a multi-functional entertainment complex that hosts concerts, club nights, cultural events, and festivals. It features several stages and spaces, making it a hub for various music genres, from pop and rock to electronic and hip-hop.

Müpa Budapest (Palace of Arts)

Müpa Budapest is a world-class cultural venue that hosts classical music concerts, opera performances, jazz shows, and contemporary music events. It's home to the Budapest Festival Orchestra and offers top-notch acoustics and a stunning architectural design.

BMC - Opus Jazz Club

The Budapest Music Center (BMC) is a cultural institution dedicated to promoting contemporary and classical music. The Opus Jazz Club, located within BMC, focuses on jazz concerts, providing an excellent platform for local and international jazz musicians.

Dürer Kert

Dürer Kert is a popular club and music venue known for its diverse music program, including rock, indie, punk, and electronic music. It has both indoor and outdoor stages and hosts live concerts as well as club nights.

Gödör Klub

Gödör Klub is an open-air venue located in the heart of Budapest. It hosts concerts, DJ performances, theater shows, and cultural events throughout the year, attracting a diverse crowd of music lovers.

Budapest Park

Budapest Park is a large outdoor concert venue that hosts major international acts, festivals, and concerts during the warmer months. It's a great place to enjoy live music in a festival-like atmosphere.

Széchenyi Thermal Bath Night Spa

The Széchenyi Thermal Bath Night Spa is a unique and popular attraction in Budapest, allowing visitors to experience the relaxing and therapeutic benefits of the thermal baths under the stars and moonlight. Here's what you need to know about the Széchenyi Thermal Bath Night Spa:

Széchenyi Thermal Bath

Széchenyi Thermal Bath is one of the largest and most famous thermal baths in Budapest. It is located in City Park (Városliget) and features a stunning Neo-Baroque architectural design. The bath's thermal waters come from natural hot springs, known for their healing properties.

Night Spa Sessions

In addition to the regular daytime operations, Széchenyi Thermal Bath offers night spa sessions a few times a week. During these special evening hours, the baths are illuminated with atmospheric lighting, creating a magical and soothing ambiance.

Opening Hours

The night spa sessions at Széchenyi Thermal Bath typically take place on Friday and Saturday nights, starting from around 10:00 PM and lasting until 3:00 AM. However, it's essential to check the official website or inquire in advance about the specific schedule, as it may vary.

Thermal Pools and Facilities

The night spa sessions provide access to various indoor and outdoor thermal pools, saunas, and steam rooms. Visitors can enjoy soaking in the warm, mineral-rich waters, which are believed to have numerous health benefits, such as relieving muscle tension and promoting relaxation.

Cocktail Bars

During the night spa sessions, you'll find cocktail bars and refreshment options available within the baths' premises. This allows you to indulge in a drink or snack while enjoying the tranquil surroundings.

Atmosphere

The night spa experience at Széchenyi Thermal Bath offers a unique and atmospheric way to unwind after a day of exploring Budapest. The combination of warm water, cool night air, and soft lighting creates a serene and rejuvenating environment.

Towel and Locker Rental

If you plan to visit the Széchenyi Thermal Bath Night Spa, you can rent towels and lockers on-site. Keep in mind that you'll need to bring your swimwear and any additional personal items you might need.

Please note that the night spa sessions can be quite popular, especially during peak tourist seasons. It's advisable to book your tickets in advance to secure your spot and avoid disappointment.

Rooftop Bars

Budapest offers a selection of rooftop bars that provide stunning panoramic views of the city's iconic landmarks and skyline. These rooftop venues are perfect for enjoying drinks, socializing, and taking in the breathtaking scenery. Here are some popular rooftop bars in Budapest:

360 Bar

Located on top of the luxurious Andrássy Hotel, 360 Bar offers a 360-degree view of Budapest's skyline. With both indoor and outdoor seating, visitors can enjoy cocktails, wines, and a variety of drinks while taking in vistas of St. Stephen's Basilica, the Danube River, and the Buda Castle District.

High Note SkyBar

Situated atop the Aria Hotel Budapest, High Note SkyBar provides a sophisticated atmosphere and panoramic views. It's an ideal spot for enjoying specialty cocktails, fine wines, and a selection of light bites while overlooking St. Stephen's Basilica and the surrounding cityscape.

St. Andrea Wine & Skybar

St. Andrea Wine & Skybar is located on the roof of a historic building near the Basilica. Besides offering a wide selection of Hungarian wines, it boasts a splendid view of St. Stephen's Basilica, Liberty Square, and the Parliament Building.

Toprum Sky & Bar

This rooftop bar, located atop Hotel Rum Budapest, offers a relaxed and laid-back atmosphere. With views of Gellért Hill and the Liberty Bridge, visitors can enjoy a range of drinks, including cocktails and local craft beers.

ÉS Deli & Bar Terrace

Situated on the top floor of the Kempinski Hotel Corvinus Budapest, the ÉS Deli & Bar Terrace provides views of the city center and the Fashion Street. It's an excellent place to unwind with refreshing beverages and enjoy the sights.

Clubbing Scene

Budapest has a vibrant and diverse clubbing scene, making it a popular destination for partygoers and music enthusiasts. The city offers a wide range of nightclubs and dance venues that cater to various music tastes and styles. Here's what you can expect from Budapest's clubbing scene:

Variety of Music

Budapest's clubbing scene caters to a wide range of music genres. You can find clubs playing everything from techno, house, and electronic dance music to hip-hop, R&B, and mainstream hits.

Whether you're into underground beats or commercial tunes, there's a club for you.

Ruin Bars with Dance Floors

Many of Budapest's famous ruin bars, known for their unique and bohemian atmosphere, also have dance floors and club nights. Szimpla Kert, Instant, and Fogas Ház are some ruin bars that transform into lively dance venues after dark.

Boat Parties

The Danube River that flows through Budapest provides a picturesque backdrop for boat parties and club nights. Party boats offer a memorable experience of dancing and socializing while cruising along the river.

Akvárium Klub

Akvárium Klub is a popular cultural and entertainment complex in Budapest that hosts various club nights and music events. It features multiple stages, including an outdoor garden area, making it a hotspot for both local and international DJs and artists.

Lärm

Lärm is an underground club known for its focus on techno and electronic music. It has a loyal following among techno enthusiasts and often hosts techno parties and events with local and international DJs.

Instant-Fogas

These two clubs, located in the same building, are famous for their vibrant and eclectic music scene. They feature multiple dance floors with different music styles, providing something for everyone in one location.

Toldi Klub

Toldi Klub is a versatile club and cultural venue known for its electronic music events, art exhibitions, film screenings, and more. It's a creative and artistic space that attracts a diverse crowd.

Corvin Club

Corvin Club is a multi-level club with various dance floors and music styles, from techno and house to drum and bass. It's a popular choice for dance music enthusiasts and often hosts international DJ performances.

EVENTS AND FESTIVALS

Budapest is a city that loves to celebrate, and throughout the year, it hosts a wide array of events and festivals that cater to various interests and tastes. From cultural celebrations and music festivals to culinary events and sports competitions, there is something for everyone. Here are some of the most notable events and festivals in Budapest:

Budapest Advent Fair

The Budapest Advent Fair, also known as the Budapest Christmas Fair, is a magical and enchanting event that takes place during the Advent season leading up to Christmas. It is one of the most popular and beloved Christmas markets in Hungary, attracting both locals and tourists from all over the world. The fair transforms the heart of the city into a winter wonderland, offering a festive and joyous atmosphere. Here's what you can expect from the Budapest Advent Fair:

Dates and Location

The Budapest Advent Fair usually starts in late November or early December and runs until December 24th, coinciding with the Advent period. The fair is held in the city center, with Vörösmarty Square being the main location.

Christmas Market Stalls

The main attraction of the Budapest Advent Fair is the numerous market stalls set up around Vörösmarty Square. These stalls offer a wide array of holiday gifts, handcrafted items, Christmas decorations, toys, and souvenirs. It's the perfect place to find unique and meaningful presents for loved ones.

Culinary Delights

The fair is a paradise for food lovers, offering a mouthwatering selection of Hungarian and international culinary treats. You can savor traditional Hungarian dishes such as chimney cake (kürtőskalács), roasted chestnuts, lángos (deep-fried flatbread), and delicious sausages.

Warm Drinks

To keep warm in the winter chill, visitors can enjoy traditional Hungarian mulled wine (forralt bor), hot fruit punch, and other warm beverages while strolling through the fair.

Christmas Decorations and Lights

The fairgrounds are beautifully adorned with twinkling lights, festive decorations, and Christmas ornaments, creating a magical and heartwarming ambiance.

Live Performances

The Budapest Advent Fair features daily live performances, including Christmas concerts, caroling choirs, folk dance shows, and theatrical performances. The entertainment adds to the festive spirit and provides joyous moments for visitors.

Santa Claus and Activities for Kids

Children will be delighted to meet Santa Claus (Mikulás in Hungarian) and participate in various kid-friendly activities, such as crafts, storytelling, and puppet shows.

Special Events

The Budapest Advent Fair often hosts special events, workshops, and programs throughout the Advent season. These may include art exhibitions, folk traditions, and interactive activities for both kids and adults.

Budapest Spring Festival

The Budapest Spring Festival, or Budapesti Tavaszi Fesztivál in Hungarian, is one of the most prominent and anticipated cultural events in the Hungarian capital. Held annually in spring, the festival showcases a diverse program of arts, music, dance, theater, and other cultural performances. It is a celebration of creativity and talent, attracting both local and international artists and audiences. Here's what you can expect from the Budapest Spring Festival:

Dates and Duration

The Budapest Spring Festival typically takes place in late March or early April and lasts for about two to three weeks. The festival's exact dates may vary each year, so it's best to check the official website or local event listings for the current schedule.

Cultural Performances

The festival offers a rich and varied program of cultural performances, featuring classical music concerts, opera and ballet performances, theater plays, contemporary dance shows, and art exhibitions. These events are held at various venues throughout Budapest, including prestigious concert halls, theaters, and galleries.

International Artists

The Budapest Spring Festival attracts renowned artists, musicians, dancers, and performers from around the world. Audiences have the opportunity to experience world-class performances in the heart of Budapest.

Hungarian Artists and Traditions

The festival also highlights Hungarian artists and cultural traditions, providing a platform for local talents to showcase their work and contributions to the arts.

Street Performances and Festivities

In addition to the ticketed events, the festival often includes free street performances, open-air concerts, and festive activities in public squares and parks. These outdoor events add to the festival's vibrant atmosphere and bring arts and culture closer to the community.

Artistic Diversity

The Budapest Spring Festival embraces artistic diversity, featuring classical masterpieces, contemporary creations, cross-genre collaborations, and innovative performances that appeal to a wide range of tastes and interests.

Thematic Programming

Each year, the festival may have a specific theme or focus that ties the performances and events together, creating a cohesive and immersive experience for attendees.

Family-Friendly Events

The festival includes family-friendly events and activities, making it a wonderful opportunity for parents to introduce their children to the arts and cultural experiences.

Budapest Wine Festival

The Budapest Wine Festival, known as "Budavári Borfesztivál" in Hungarian, is one of Hungary's most celebrated wine events. Held annually in the historic setting of Buda Castle, this festival showcases the country's rich winemaking traditions, offering a unique and delightful experience for wine enthusiasts and visitors alike. Here's what you can expect from the Budapest Wine Festival:

Dates and Location

The Budapest Wine Festival typically takes place in early September, spanning over four days. The event is hosted at Buda Castle, a UNESCO World Heritage Site, providing a picturesque backdrop for the wine festivities.

Hungarian Wines

The festival primarily focuses on Hungarian wines, allowing visitors to sample a vast array of wine varietals from different regions of Hungary. You'll have the opportunity to taste renowned Hungarian wines, including whites, reds, rosés, and sweet wines.

Wine Producers and Cellars

The festival brings together numerous winemakers and wine cellars from all over Hungary. Each participating winery showcases its best wines, and visitors can interact with the winemakers themselves, learning about the winemaking process and the stories behind their creations.

Wine Tasting

The Budapest Wine Festival offers various tasting opportunities, allowing you to purchase tasting tickets or wine passes that grant access to different wine tasting booths. It's an excellent way to explore the diverse and exquisite flavors of Hungarian wines.

Gastronomy

The festival is not only about wine; it also celebrates Hungarian gastronomy. You can enjoy delicious Hungarian dishes and delicacies, such as lángos (deep-fried flatbread), sausages, traditional stews, and other specialties that complement the wine offerings.

Cultural Performances

The Budapest Wine Festival also features cultural performances, live music, folk dance shows, and entertainment, creating a lively and festive atmosphere for attendees.

Wine Education

For those interested in learning more about wine, the festival often hosts wine seminars, workshops, and presentations led by experts, allowing visitors to deepen their knowledge and appreciation of Hungarian wines.

Souvenirs and Crafts: In addition to wine and food, the festival also offers craft stalls and souvenir shops where you can purchase unique gifts and mementos.

Sziget Festival

Sziget Festival, often referred to as the "Island of Freedom," is one of Europe's largest and most renowned music and cultural festivals. Held annually in Budapest, Hungary, on Óbudai Island in the middle of the Danube River, Sziget Festival offers a diverse and eclectic program that attracts hundreds of thousands of visitors from all over the world. Here's what you can expect from the Sziget Festival:

Dates and Duration

Sziget Festival usually takes place in August and lasts for seven days, making it a week-long celebration of music, arts, and culture.

Music Performances

The festival features a star-studded lineup of international and local musicians, encompassing various music genres. From rock and pop to electronic dance music, hip-hop, indie, and world music, Sziget caters to diverse musical tastes.

Main Stages and Thematic Venues

Sziget Festival offers several main stages where headlining acts perform, along with thematic venues and smaller stages showcasing lesser-known artists and alternative music styles.

International Artists

Sziget attracts some of the biggest names in the music industry, including global superstars and critically acclaimed bands and artists. Past headliners have included Ed Sheeran, Foo Fighters, Rihanna, Muse, and many others.

A38 Stage

The A38 Stage, located on a converted Ukrainian stone-carrier ship, is a highlight of Sziget Festival. It hosts a variety of music acts, especially alternative and electronic artists.

Cultural Program

Besides music, Sziget offers an extensive cultural program, including art exhibitions, theater performances, circus shows, dance workshops, and interactive installations. The festival aims to create a vibrant and immersive experience beyond just music.

World Music

Sziget embraces world music, providing a platform for musicians and artists from different cultures and countries to perform, promoting cultural diversity and understanding.

Art and Installations

The festival site is adorned with various art installations, sculptures, and colorful decorations, adding to the festival's unique atmosphere.

Camping and Community

Sziget is known for its vibrant camping scene, with festival-goers setting up tents and forming a lively and friendly community on the island.

Island of Freedom

Sziget's motto is the "Island of Freedom," symbolizing its commitment to inclusivity, acceptance, and open-mindedness. The festival aims to create a space where people from different backgrounds can come together and celebrate unity and diversity.

Budapest International Documentary Festival (BIDF)

The Budapest International Documentary Festival (BIDF) is an annual event that celebrates the art of documentary filmmaking. It provides a platform for filmmakers to showcase thought-provoking and insightful documentaries from around the world. The festival aims to promote documentary films as a powerful medium for storytelling, raising awareness, and exploring various social, cultural, and political issues. Here are some key features of the Budapest International Documentary Festival:

Dates and Duration

The BIDF usually takes place in January or February and lasts for several days, with screenings and events held throughout the festival's duration.

Film Selection

The festival curates a diverse selection of documentary films, encompassing various genres, styles, and themes. These films often touch on pressing global issues, personal stories, environmental concerns, historical events, and more.

International Filmmakers

BIDF attracts filmmakers from different parts of the world, providing an opportunity for them to showcase their work to a broad and engaged audience.

Competitive Categories

The festival may have competitive categories for documentaries, where selected films compete for awards and recognition. Jury panels comprising industry professionals and experts evaluate the films and select winners in various categories.

Special Screenings and Retrospectives

In addition to the competition, BIDF may feature special screenings of acclaimed documentary films and retrospectives of renowned filmmakers, paying homage to their contributions to the genre.

Q&A Sessions and Discussions

Following some screenings, the festival often hosts Q&A sessions with filmmakers and subjects, giving the audience a chance to gain deeper insights into the films and their production.

Industry Events

BIDF may also include industry-related events, such as masterclasses, workshops, and panel discussions, providing valuable networking and educational opportunities for filmmakers and professionals in the documentary industry.

Venues

Screenings and events take place at various venues across Budapest, including cinemas, theaters, cultural centers, and art spaces.

Budapest Pride

Budapest Pride is an annual LGBT+ (Lesbian, Gay, Bisexual, Transgender, and other sexual and gender minorities) event held in Budapest, Hungary. It is a celebration of diversity, inclusion, and LGBTQ+ rights, providing a platform for the community and its allies to come together, raise awareness, and advocate for equal rights and acceptance. Budapest Pride is not only a festive occasion but also a demonstration of solidarity and visibility for the LGBTQ+ community in Hungary. Here are some key features of Budapest Pride:

Dates and Duration

Budapest Pride typically takes place in June or July, coinciding with LGBTQ+ Pride Month celebrated worldwide. The main parade and events usually span over several days, with various cultural, educational, and social activities.

Pride Parade

The highlight of Budapest Pride is the Pride Parade, where thousands of participants march through the streets of Budapest, proudly displaying rainbow flags, banners, and placards. The parade is a symbol of unity, diversity, and the fight for equality.

Cultural and Social Events

Budapest Pride includes a diverse program of cultural events, such as film screenings, art exhibitions, theater performances, concerts, parties, and community gatherings. These events aim to celebrate LGBTQ+ culture and provide opportunities for networking and socializing.

Advocacy and Awareness

Budapest Pride also serves as a platform for raising awareness about LGBTQ+ rights and issues. It provides an opportunity to address discrimination, promote understanding, and advocate for legal protections and social acceptance.

LGBTQ+ Visibility

The festival fosters visibility for the LGBTQ+ community, encouraging individuals to embrace their identities openly and without fear. It also serves as a positive and empowering experience for young LGBTQ+ individuals who may be struggling with self-acceptance.

Allyship and Support

Budapest Pride welcomes allies—friends, family members, and supporters of the LGBTQ+ community—to join in the celebration and stand in solidarity with the cause of equality and human rights.

Safety and Security

The organizers of Budapest Pride work closely with local authorities to ensure the safety and security of participants and attendees during the events.

International Support

Budapest Pride receives support from various international organizations and activists, further strengthening its message of inclusivity and equality.

National Gallop

The National Gallop, known as "Nemzeti Vágta" in Hungarian, is a prestigious equestrian event held annually in Budapest, Hungary. It celebrates the country's rich equestrian heritage, showcasing traditional Hungarian horsemanship, folklore, and cultural traditions. The event attracts thousands of spectators and participants, making it one of the most anticipated equestrian festivals in Hungary. Here's what you can expect from the National Gallop:

Dates and Location

The National Gallop is typically held in September, and the exact dates may vary from year to year. The event takes place in Heroes' Square (Hősök tere), one of Budapest's iconic landmarks and a symbol of Hungarian history and identity.

Equestrian Races

The highlight of the National Gallop is the horse racing competitions, featuring skilled riders and beautiful horses. The races showcase various equestrian disciplines, including flat racing, show jumping, and carriage racing.

Regional Teams

The races are organized as a team competition, with teams representing different regions of Hungary. Each team consists of local riders and horses, adding a competitive and regional element to the event.

Opening Parade

The National Gallop begins with a grand opening parade, featuring riders in traditional Hungarian costumes, historical reenactments, and folk music and dance performances.

Traditional Equestrian Skills

In addition to the races, the National Gallop includes demonstrations of traditional equestrian skills, such as archery on horseback and mounted spear throwing, showcasing Hungary's historical equestrian heritage.

Cultural and Folklore Programs

The festival offers a range of cultural and folklore programs, celebrating Hungarian traditions, arts, and crafts. Visitors can enjoy live music performances, traditional dance shows, artisan markets, and exhibitions of Hungarian cultural heritage.

Family-Friendly Activities

The National Gallop is a family-friendly event, with activities and entertainment for children, such as pony rides and interactive programs.

National Gallop Fair: Surrounding the main event area, there is a National Gallop Fair featuring food stalls, handicraft vendors, and traditional Hungarian delicacies, making it a vibrant and lively atmosphere.

Formula 1 Hungarian Grand Prix

The Formula 1 Hungarian Grand Prix is an annual motorsport event held in Hungary as part of the Formula 1 World Championship. It is one of the most prestigious and long-standing races on the Formula 1 calendar. The race takes place at the Hungaroring, a motorsport circuit located near the city of Budapest. Here are some key features of the Formula 1 Hungarian Grand Prix:

Dates

The Hungarian Grand Prix typically takes place in the summer, usually in late July or early August. The exact date may vary from year to year, depending on the Formula 1 calendar.

Hungaroring Circuit

The race is held at the Hungaroring, a circuit known for its tight and twisty layout. The track's lack of long straights and numerous tight corners make it physically demanding for the drivers and challenging for overtaking, providing exciting and intense racing action.

F1 World Championship

The Hungarian Grand Prix is part of the Formula 1 World Championship, a series of races held in different countries around the globe. Drivers and teams compete for points to win the championship titles.

Fan Attendance

The Hungarian Grand Prix attracts a large number of fans from Hungary and around the world. Spectators come to witness the adrenaline-pumping racing and support their favorite drivers and teams.

Entertainment and Activities

In addition to the on-track action, the Hungarian Grand Prix offers various entertainment and activities for fans, including concerts, autograph sessions, and displays of vintage cars.

Surrounding Events

Beyond the race itself, the Hungarian Grand Prix provides an opportunity for visitors to explore Budapest and experience the city's vibrant culture, history, and attractions.

Accessible Location

The Hungaroring circuit is located about 20 kilometers northeast of Budapest, making it easily accessible for both local and international visitors.

Racing Legends

Over the years, the Hungarian Grand Prix has seen many racing legends competing and achieving memorable victories, adding to the race's historical significance.

Budapest Christmas Tram

The Budapest Christmas Tram, also known as "Karácsonyi villamos" in Hungarian, is a festive and magical tradition that takes place during the Christmas season in Budapest, Hungary. The city's iconic trams are adorned with thousands of twinkling lights and festive decorations, transforming them into enchanting Christmas trams. Here's what you can expect from the Budapest Christmas Tram:

Dates and Duration

The Budapest Christmas Tram usually starts operating in late November and continues until early January. The exact dates may vary slightly from year to year.

Decorated Trams

Several trams in the city's public transportation fleet are specially decorated for the Christmas season. These trams are adorned with colorful lights, wreaths, ornaments, and other festive decorations, creating a cheerful and heartwarming ambiance.

Festive Routes

The Christmas trams operate on various tram lines throughout Budapest. They pass through some of the city's most iconic landmarks and main streets, providing passengers with a scenic and joyful ride.

Evening Rides

The Christmas Trams are particularly enchanting during the evening and night when the lights create a magical atmosphere as they traverse the city's streets.

Popular Photo Spots

The Christmas Trams have become popular photo spots for both locals and tourists. Many people gather at designated tram stops or busy areas to capture pictures of the beautifully decorated trams.

Holiday Spirit

The Christmas Trams add to the festive spirit of Budapest during the holiday season, making the city feel even more charming and inviting.

Regular Public Transportation

While the Christmas Trams are decorated for the holiday season, they continue to operate as regular public transportation vehicles. Passengers can hop on and off the trams as usual while enjoying the festive decorations.

MAPS

Budapest Map

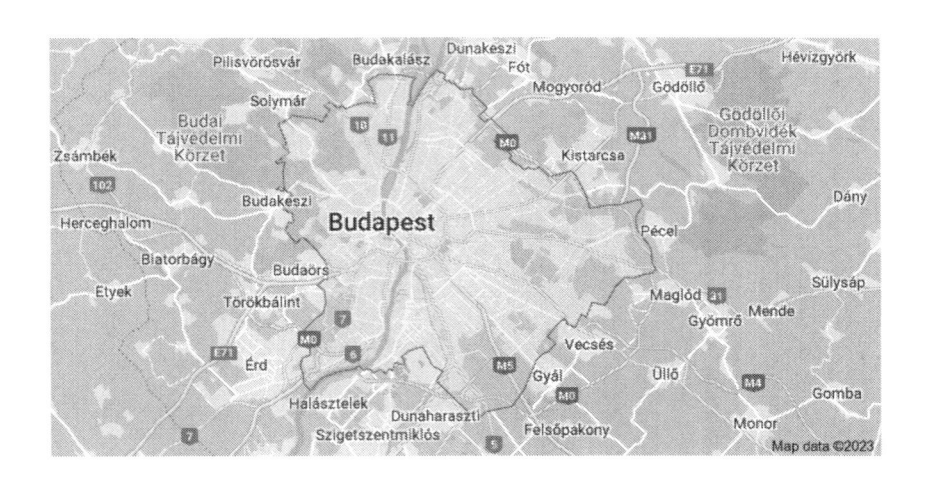

Budapest Travel Guide 2023 and Beyond

Sziget Festival Map

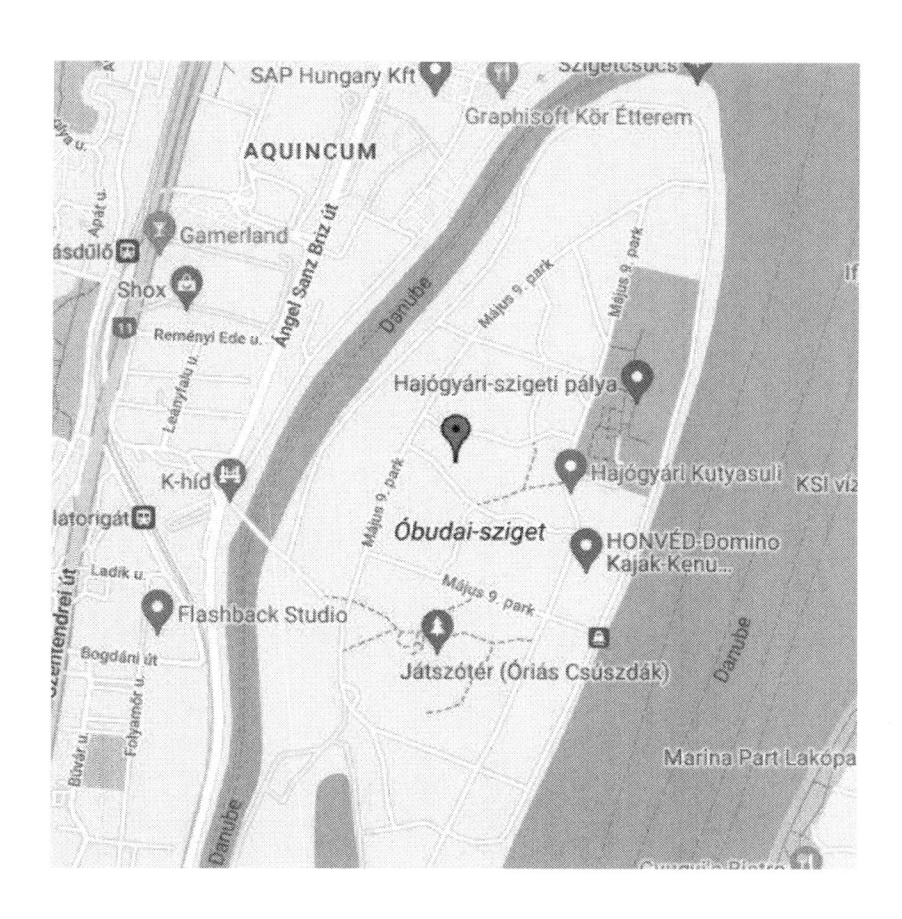

Aliz Kristof

Budapest Christmas Market Map

Budapest Travel Guide 2023 and Beyond

Budapest Museums Map

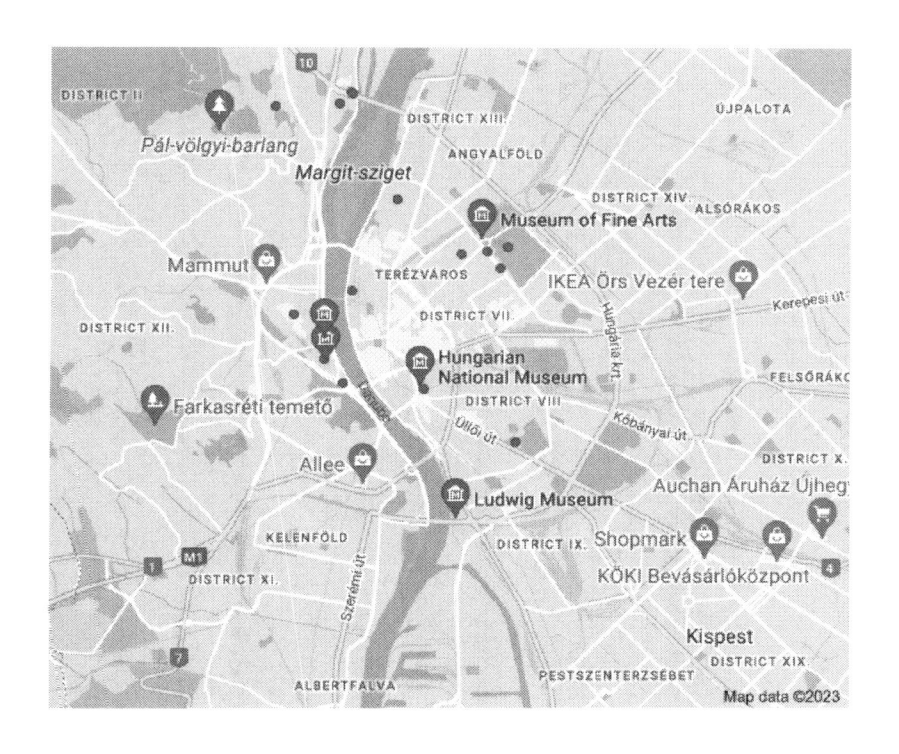

Aliz Kristof

Széchenyi Thermal Bath map

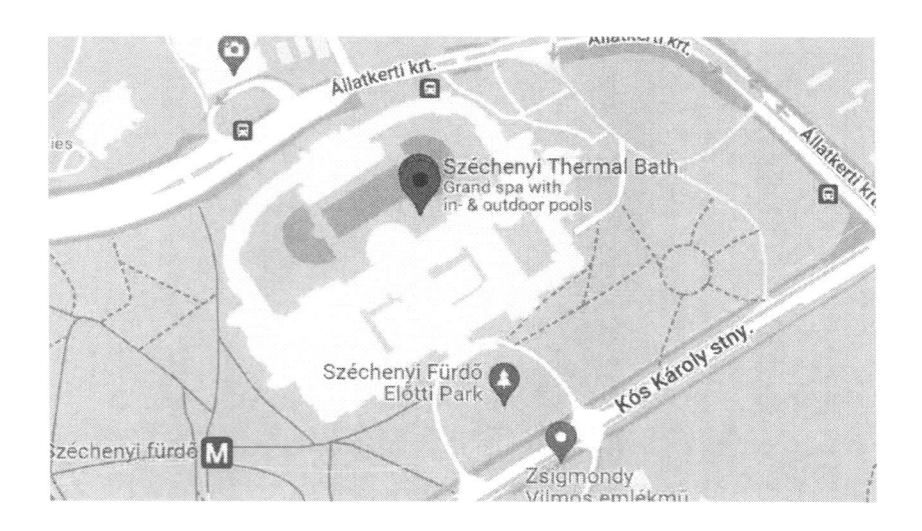

Budapest Travel Guide 2023 and Beyond

Restaurants Map

ITINERARIES

Historical and Cultural Exploration (3 Days)

Day 1

Morning: Visit Buda Castle, explore the historic Castle District, and enjoy panoramic views of the city from Fisherman's Bastion.

Afternoon: Head to Matthias Church and take a guided tour to learn about its rich history and architectural significance.

Evening: Wander along the Danube Promenade and admire the iconic Chain Bridge and the Parliament building beautifully illuminated at night.

Day 2

Morning: Visit the Hungarian National Museum and immerse yourself in the country's history and cultural heritage.

Afternoon: Explore Heroes' Square and City Park. Visit the Museum of Fine Arts or relax in the park's serene surroundings.

Evening: Attend a traditional Hungarian folk dance performance or classical music concert.

Day 3

Morning: Visit the House of Terror Museum to learn about Hungary's dark past during Nazi and Soviet regimes.

Afternoon: Explore the Jewish Quarter, including the Dohány Street Synagogue, the Great Market Hall, and Kazinczy Street with its vibrant street art.

Evening: Relax and unwind in one of Budapest's famous thermal baths, such as Széchenyi or Gellért Baths.

Family-Friendly Fun (4 Days)

Day 1

Morning: Visit the Budapest Zoo and Botanical Garden, home to a wide variety of animals and beautiful plant exhibits.

Afternoon: Head to Margaret Island and enjoy a family picnic, rent bicycles, or explore the musical fountain show.

Evening: Take a Danube River cruise with dinner and enjoy the city's landmarks from the water.

Day 2

Morning: Visit the Palace of Miracles, a hands-on science museum designed for kids.

Afternoon: Head to Városliget, where kids can enjoy the Children's Railway or the boating lake.

Evening: Relax at a family-friendly restaurant or explore the fun-filled Tropicarium, featuring an impressive aquarium.

Day 3

Morning: Visit the Hungarian Railway History Park, where kids can explore vintage trains and learn about railway history.

Afternoon: Enjoy an exciting treasure hunt tour or a guided bike tour designed for families.

Evening: Attend a puppet show or a family-friendly performance at a theater.

Day 4

Morning: Take a day trip to Aquaworld Budapest, a thrilling water park with slides and pools suitable for all ages.

Afternoon: Explore City Park and enjoy a ride on the Budapest Eye ferris wheel.

Evening: Visit a sweet shop for traditional Hungarian treats like kürtőskalács (chimney cake) or lángos.

Culinary Delights (2 Days)

Day 1

Morning: Start your day with a visit to the Central Market Hall to taste local produce and Hungarian specialties.

Afternoon: Take a food tour through the Jewish Quarter, sampling traditional dishes like goulash and chimney cake.

Evening: Dine at a traditional Hungarian restaurant and savor dishes like chicken paprikash or töltött káposzta (stuffed cabbage).

Day 2

Morning: Explore the Belváros-Lipótváros district and have breakfast at a café known for its pastries and coffee.

Afternoon: Take a wine tasting tour in the wine cellars of Buda Castle or visit one of the wine bars in the city.

Evening: Try a tasting menu at a Michelin-starred restaurant for a gourmet experience.

Romantic Getaway (3 Days)

Day 1

Morning: Take a romantic stroll along the Danube Promenade and cross the Chain Bridge to enjoy views of the Parliament building.

Afternoon: Visit Várkert Bazaar and relax in the beautiful garden with views of the Castle District.

Evening: Take a sunset cruise on the Danube River and enjoy a candlelit dinner on board.

Day 2

Morning: Visit the historical Vajdahunyad Castle and explore the romantic surroundings of City Park.

Afternoon: Take a horse-drawn carriage ride through the historic streets of Budapest.

Evening: Enjoy a private riverfront dinner with a view of the illuminated city.

Day 3

Morning: Relax at one of Budapest's famous thermal baths, such as Rudas Bath or Lukács Bath.

Afternoon: Take a leisurely boat ride on Margaret Island and have a picnic in a secluded spot.

Evening: End your romantic getaway with a romantic walk along the Danube under the twinkling lights of the city.

Budget-Friendly Budapest (4 Days)

Day 1

Morning: Explore the Castle District, including Fisherman's Bastion, where you can enjoy stunning views for free.

Afternoon: Take a self-guided walking tour of the Jewish Quarter to see its landmarks and street art.

Evening: Have dinner at a local street food vendor or explore the many affordable eateries in the city.

Day 2

Morning: Visit the Hungarian National Museum, where entrance fees are reasonable, to learn about the country's history.

Afternoon: Head to Gellért Hill for panoramic views of the city and a visit to the Citadel.

Evening: Enjoy a budget-friendly river cruise without dinner to see the city lights from the water.

Day 3

Morning: Visit Heroes' Square and City Park, where you can explore for free.

Afternoon: Relax at one of Budapest's free thermal baths, such as the Széchenyi Park Baths.

Evening: Attend a free concert or event at one of the city's squares or parks.

Day 4

Morning: Explore the vibrant and bohemian district of Erzsébetváros, known for its art scene and unique shops.

Afternoon: Take a leisurely walk along Andrássy Avenue, window shopping and admiring the historic buildings.

Evening: End your budget-friendly trip with a picnic in a park or by the Danube, enjoying the scenic beauty without spending a dime.

CONCLUSION

Budapest is a city that leaves a lasting impression on all who visit. Its majestic architecture, stunning landmarks, and warm hospitality make it a must-visit destination. As you explore the historic splendor of Buda Castle, relax in the rejuvenating thermal baths, marvel at the grandeur of the Hungarian Parliament, and indulge in the mouthwatering Hungarian cuisine, you'll find yourself immersed in the beauty and charm of this magnificent city. Whether you're strolling along the Danube River, wandering through the vibrant neighborhoods, or uncovering hidden gems, Budapest will continue to surprise and delight you with its timeless appeal. So pack your bags and get ready to embark on an unforgettable journey to Budapest, where history, culture, and gastronomy intertwine to create an extraordinary travel experience.

INDEX

Andrassy Avenue   32
Anonymous Statue (Ismeretlen Írók Tere)   88
Army Statues   82
Batthyány Square Metro Station   124
Best Restaurants   53
Buda Castle   57
Buda Castle Labyrinth   118
Budapest advent fair   163
Budapest Christmas Market Map   180
Budapest Christmas Tram   176
Budapest Ferris Wheel   25
Budapest International Documentary Festival (BIDF)   170
Budapest Map   178
Budapest Museums Map   181
Budapest Palace of Arts (Müpa Budapest)   74
Budapest Pride   171
Budapest Spring Festival   165
Budapest Wine Festival   166
Budget Accomodations   47
Budget-Friendly Budapest (4 Days)   187
Chain Bridge   26
Church of Our Lady (Boldogasszony-templom) in Óbuda   137
Citadella   42
Clubbing Scene   161
Culinary Delights (2 Days)   185
Cultural Etiquette   19

Currency 11
Danube River Cruises 38
Déli Railway Station Tunnel 126
District IX (Ferencváros) 141
District V (Belváros-Lipótváros) 142
District VI (Terézváros) 142
District VII (Erzsébetváros) 141
District VII (Jewish Quarter) 143
District VIII (Józsefváros) 141
District XIII (Újlipótváros) 142
Dohány Street Synagogue 67
Dress Code 21
Ecseri Flea Market (Ecseri Piac) 100
Emergency Numbers 23
Family-Friendly Fun (4 Days) 184
Fény Street Market (Fény utcai Piac) 101
Ferenc Liszt Monument 93
Formula 1 Hungarian Grand Prix 174
Gellért Baths 63
Gozsdu Courtyard 146
Great Market Hall 97
Great Market Hall (Nagyvásárcsarnok) 68
Great Synagogue (Dohány Street Synagogue) 133
Heroes' Square 30
Historical and Cultural Exploration (3 Days) 184
Hold Street Market Hall (Hold utcai Piac) 95
Holocaust Memorial Center 111
Hospital in the Rock Nuclear Bunker Museum 114
House of Terror 113
Hungarian National Gallery 107
Hungarian National Museum 104
Hungarian Parliament 59
Hungarian State Opera House 70
Imre Nagy Memorial 78
Kazinczy Street 145

Language   12
Lehel Market (Lehel tér)   99
Little Princess (Kiskirálylány)   89
Live Music Venues   157
Lucury Accomodations   46
Margaret Bridge   40
Margaret Island Water Tower   34
Matthias Church (Mátyás-templom)   130
Matthias Fountain (Mátyás Kútja)   87
Millennium Underground   123
Museum of Applied Arts   109
Museum of Fine Arts   106
National Gallop   173
Opening Hours   22
Origin and History of Budapest   8
Popular Locations   45
Pub Crawls   155
Public Transportation   15
Restaurants Map   183
Romantic Getaway (3 Days)   186
Ronald Reagan Statue   91
Rooftop Bars   160
Ruin Bars   154
Ruin Bars Street Art   148
Safety   16
Shoes on the Danube Bank   85
St. Anne's Church (Szent Anna-templom)   134
St. Elizabeth of Hungary Church (Erzsébet-templom)   139
St. Michael's Church (Szent Mihály-templom)   136
St. Stephen's Basilica (Szent István Bazilika)   128
St. Stephen's Basilica Architecture   65
Steve Jobs Memorial Statue   80
Street Art Festivals   151
Széchenyi Chain Bridge   61
Széchenyi Thermal Bath map   182

Széchenyi Thermal Bath Night Spa   158
Szemlőhegyi Cave   120
Sziget Festival   168
Sziget Festival Map   179
Tap Water   18
The innovative Whale (Bálna Budapest)   76
The Statue of Liberty (Szabadság Szobor)   83
Thermal Baths   28
Tipping   18
Travel Insurance   14
Tunnel under Castle Hill   121
Urban Art Galleries   149
Vajdahunyad Castle   36
Vajdahunyad Castle Architecture   72
Visa Requirements   10
Weather   13
What to eat   49
Where to eat   51

Printed in Great Britain
by Amazon